Contents

Mini nut roasts with candied carrots 5
Teriyaki sauce 6
Pasta e fagioli 7
Vegetable tagine with apricot quinoa 8
Sri Lankan braised roots stew & coconut dhal dumplings 10
Roasted cauli-broc bowl with tahini hummus 13
Griddled vegetables with melting aubergines 13
Kung pao-style cauliflower & kidney beans 14
Fluffy almond pancakes with blueberry ripple yogurt 16
Luxury hummus 17
Roasted root veg traybake 18
Staffordshire oatcakes with mushrooms 19
Rhubarb gin 20
Miso aubergines 21
Veggie olive wraps with mustard vinaigrette 22
Basic lentils 22
Seitan & black bean stir-fry 23
Chapatis 25
Tarka dhal 25
Saag aloo 26
Tomato bruschetta 27
Avocado hummus & crudités 28
Garlicky mushroom penne 29
Vegetarian Thai green curry 30
Chilli-charred Brussels sprouts 31
Lentil ragu with courgetti 32

- Turmeric latte 33
- Squash & cabbage sabzi 33
- Kentucky fried seitan 34
- Spiced aubergine bake 36
- Spring tabbouleh 38
- Hummus 38
- Beetroot, hummus & crispy chickpea sub sandwich 39
- Chocolate & date tart 40
- Squash & spinach fusilli with pecans 41
- Curried cashew dip 42
- Spiced roast cauliflower with herby rice 43
- Veggie protein chilli 44
- Date butter 45
- Walnut & almond muesli with grated apple 45
- Celeriac, hazelnut & truffle soup 46
- Gnocchi with herb sauce 47
- Curried parsnip soup shots 48
- Roasted stuffed cauliflower 49
- Cauliflower, squash, coconut & lentil curry 51
- Barbecue sesame sweet potatoes 52
- Quick hummus 53
- Kidney bean curry 53
- Thai red curry with quick pickled cucumber 54
- Brussels sprouts pad Thai 57
- Cocoa & cherry oat bake 58
- Raspberry ripple chia pudding 58
- Crispy sweet potatoes with chickpeas & tahini yogurt 59
- Peach iced tea 60

Avocado on toast	61
Red pepper & bean tikka masala	62
Pear, pumpkin & ginger juice mocktail	63
Slow cooker ratatouille	63
Leek, pea & watercress soup	64
Crunchy parsnips	65
Avocado & cannellini bean dip	66
Sweet potato, peanut butter & chilli quesadillas	67
Pumpkin seed butter	68
Spinach & chickpea dhal	68
Parsnip gnocchi	69
Chilli & avocado salsa sweet potatoes	70
Fruity mocktail	71
Cranberry & lentil bake	72
Nut roast	73
Chilli tempeh stir-fry	75
Autumn vegetable salad with saffron dressing	76
Squash steaks with chestnut & cavolo nero pilaf	77
Roast asparagus bowls with tahini lemon dressing	78
Sweet potato & black bean chilli with zesty quinoa	79
Peanut butter overnight oats	80
Barley & broccoli risotto with lemon & basil	81
Roasted root & chickpea salad	82
Chive waffles with maple & soy mushrooms	83
Creamy squash linguine	84
Sourdough starter	85
Carrot & caraway crackers	86
Curried tofu wraps	87

Aubergine & chickpea bites 88

Sticky tofu with noodles 89

Fruit leather 90

Easy bread rolls 92

Raspberry tea ice lollies 93

Piccalilli potato salad 93

Miso roasted tofu with sweet potato 94

Carrot & cumin hummus with swirled harissa 95

Pea-camole 96

Artichoke & aubergine rice 97

Really easy roasted red pepper sauce 98

Vegan coleslaw 98

Rice & peas 99

Homemade sourdough bread 100

Sizzled sprouts with pistachios & pomegranate 101

Summer porridge 102

Miso soup 103

Miso ramen 104

Root veg lentil bowl with herb pistou 105

Pitta bread 106

Cardamom & peach quinoa porridge 107

Fajita seasoning 108

Next level ratatouille 108

Spiced mushroom & lentil hotpot 110

Tofu brekkie pancakes 111

Sunshine lollies 112

Roasted squash & red onion with pistachios 113

Savoury spiced granola 113

Beetroot hummus party platter..114

Mini nut roasts with candied carrots

Prep: 35 mins **Cook:** 40 mins

Serves 6

Ingredients

- 250g bunch thin baby carrots
- 3 tbsp olive oil , plus extra for the tin
- 5 tbsp maple syrup
- 2 tbsp milled flaxseed
- 1 large onion , finely chopped
- 1 celery stick, finely chopped
- 2 garlic cloves , chopped
- 350g mixed mushrooms , finely chopped
- 3 rosemary sprigs, leaves picked and finely chopped
- 1 tsp tomato purée
- 2 tsp tamari or dark soy sauce
- 1 tbsp smoked paprika
- 100g pecans
- 50g hazelnuts
- 400g can green lentils , drained
- 400g can chickpeas , drained
- 40g ground almonds
- handful of sage and thyme leaves

You will need

- 6 mini loaf tins (silicone ones work well)

Method

STEP 1

Heat the oven to 200C/180C fan/gas 6. Scrub and trim the carrots, and cut them in half lengthways or into quarters if large. Toss the carrots with 1 tbsp olive oil and 2 tbsp maple syrup in a bowl. Season well, and tip onto a baking tray. Roast for 20-25 mins until tender and starting to caramelise.

STEP 2

Meanwhile, mix the flaxseed with 4 tbsp water and leave to thicken. Heat 1 tbsp olive oil in a frying pan, and fry the onion and celery until soft and translucent, about 10 mins. Add a splash of water if you need to, to stop them from catching. Stir in the garlic, mushrooms, rosemary, tomato purée, tamari and paprika, and fry for another 10 mins until the mushrooms are tender. Remove from the heat and leave in a bowl to cool slightly.

STEP 3

Put the pecans and hazelnuts in a food processor and blitz until roughly chopped. Add the lentils and chickpeas and blend again until you get a thick, dry paste.

STEP 4

Combine the nuts and pulses, mushroom mixture, ground almonds, 2 tbsp maple syrup and soaked flaxseed in a bowl with a good amount of seasoning. Mix everything well using your hands.

STEP 5

Oil six holes of a mini loaf tin and line each with a strip of baking parchment. Trim and cut the carrots to fit in the base in a snug single layer, cut-side down. Roughly chop any remaining carrots and mix them through the nut roast mixture. Pack it firmly into the tins and smooth over. Bake, uncovered, for 20 mins. Leave to rest for 10 mins before inverting onto a serving plate, or plates. Fry the sage and thyme in the remaining 1 tbsp olive oil until crisp, then stir through the remaining 1 tbsp maple syrup. Spoon over the nut roasts to serve.

Teriyaki sauce

Prep: 5 mins **Cook:** 10 mins

Makes 1 medium sized jar

Ingredients

- 85g light brown soft sugar

- 70ml light soy sauce
- 1 large garlic clove, crushed
- 4cm piece ginger, peeled and finely grated
- 1 tbsp cornflour
- 1 tbsp rice wine vinegar

To serve

- sesame seeds (optional)
- 2 spring onions, finely sliced (optional)

Method

STEP 1

Pour 350ml water into a small saucepan with the sugar, soy sauce, garlic and ginger. Slowly bring to a simmer, stirring occasionally until the sugar has dissolved. Cook for 5 mins more or until glossy and slightly thickened. Combine the cornflour with 1 tbsp water and quickly whisk through the sauce. Whisk through the rice wine vinegar. If it's still too thick, add a splash more water. Pour into a clean jar and leave to cool at room temperature.

STEP 2

Once cooled, will keep in the fridge for up to 1 week. Sprinkle with sesame seeds and spring onions just before serving, if you like.

Pasta e fagioli

Prep: 20 mins **Cook:** 7 hrs - 9 hrs

Serves 6 - 8

Ingredients

- 200g dried borlotti or cannellini beans , soaked for 6-8 hours
- 2 onions , cut into 1cm chunks
- 2 medium carrots , cut into 1cm chunks
- 3 celery stalks, cut into 1cm chunks
- 2 tbsp extra virgin olive oil , plus extra to serve (optional)
- 4 garlic cloves , crushed

- 1 litre fresh vegetable stock
- 400g can plum tomatoes
- 2 tbsp brown rice miso
- 6 rosemary sprigs
- 4 bay leaves
- 150g ditaloni rigati or other small pasta shapes
- 200g cavolo nero , stalks finely chopped and leaves torn
- 30g vegan parmesan , grated, to serve (optional)

Method

STEP 1

Drain the beans and bring to the boil in a pan of salted water. Cook for 10 mins, drain, rinse and put in a slow cooker with the onions, carrots and celery.

STEP 2

Stir in the olive oil, garlic, stock, tomatoes, half a can of water and the miso. Tie the herbs together with kitchen string and add these as well. Season. Cover and cook on low for 6-8 hrs, until the beans are cooked through and all of the veg is really tender.

STEP 3

Remove and discard the herbs and stir in the pasta. Cover and cook on high for another 30 mins. Add the cavolo nero stalks and leaves and cook for a final 30-40 mins, or until the pasta is cooked through and the greens are tender. Serve scattered with the cheese and drizzled with a little more olive oil, if you like.

Vegetable tagine with apricot quinoa

Prep: 30 mins **Cook:** 45 mins

Serves 4

Ingredients

For the tagine

- 1 tsp coconut oil or olive oil
- 1 red onion , chopped

- 2 garlic cloves, crushed
- ½ butternut squash (500g), chopped into large chunks
- 2 red peppers, chopped
- 400g can chickpeas, drained
- 400g can chopped tomatoes
- 500ml vegan vegetable stock (such as Marigold Vegan Bouillon Powder)
- 1 tsp ground cinnamon
- 1 tsp ground cumin
- 2 tsp turmeric
- 2 tsp paprika
- small bunch coriander, chopped
- small bunch mint, chopped, plus extra to serve
- pomegranate seeds, to serve (optional)

For the apricot quinoa

- 280g quinoa
- 80g dried apricots, chopped
- 20g flaked almonds, toasted

For the dressing

- 4 tbsp tahini
- 2 tsp preserved lemon, finely chopped, plus 2 tsp liquid from the jar
- 6 tbsp almond milk

Method

STEP 1

Heat the oil in a large frying pan and fry the onion over a medium heat for 3 mins. Add the garlic and butternut squash, and cook for a further 7 mins.

STEP 2

Add the remaining vegetables and continue to fry for 3 mins before adding the chickpeas, tomatoes and stock, along with the spices and seasoning. Simmer for 30 mins, uncovered. Meanwhile, put 750ml water in a small saucepan, bring to a simmer, then add the quinoa and cook for 20 mins. When cooked, stir in the apricots and almonds, plus a pinch of salt.

STEP 3

To make the tahini dressing, whisk together all the ingredients in a small bowl. Season with a pinch of salt.

STEP 4

Serve the quinoa with the tagine, and drizzle the tahini dressing over the top. Scatter over some chopped coriander and mint and the pomegranate seeds, if using, to finish.

Sri Lankan braised roots stew & coconut dhal dumplings

Prep: 45 mins **Cook:** 40 mins

Serves 4 - 6

Ingredients

- 1 tbsp coconut oil
- 1 tsp mustard seeds
- 6 curry leaves
- 1 onion , finely sliced
- 1 leek , finely sliced
- 3 garlic cloves , 1 sliced, 2 minced
- 2 chillies , deseeded and finely chopped
- 2 celery stalk , diced
- 1 tbsp roasted curry powder (see below)
- 400ml can chopped tomatoes
- 2 raw beetroot , peeled and cut into batons
- 3 parsnips , sliced
- 3 carrots , sliced
- 400ml can coconut milk

For the dumplings

- 100g split red lentils
- 1½ tbsp coconut oil
- 1 tsp mustard seeds
- 1 tbsp curry leaves

- 75g self-raising flour
- ½ green chilli , finely chopped
- ½ red onion , finely chopped
- 1 tsp turmeric
- 1 tsp red chilli powder
- 80g desiccated coconut
- ½ lime , juiced

For the Sri Lankan curry powder

- 10g basmati rice
- 20g coriander seeds
- 15g cumin seeds
- 10g black peppercorns
- 5g fenugreek seeds
- 3g cloves
- seeds from cardamom pods

To serve

- sliced spring onion
- fresh coriander leaves

Method

STEP 1

To make the curry powder: In a dry frying pan, toast the rice until it's browning, then add all the spices and toast for 3-5 mins until darkish brown but not burned. Blitz it all in a spice grinder, or crush with a pestle and mortar, then pass through a sieve into a jar or airtight container. Will keep for 2-3 weeks.

STEP 2

Heat the oil in a wok. Scatter in the mustard seeds and curry leaves. When they sizzle, add the onion, leek, garlic, chilli, celery and a pinch of salt, and cook, stirring, for 8-10 mins until the onion starts to colour. Add the curry powder and cook for 1 min more, then add the tomatoes, veg, coconut milk, a tsp of salt and 200ml water. Bring to the boil, cover and simmer for 10-15 mins until the veg are tender.

STEP 3

For the dumplings, boil the lentils in a pan of water until just cooked, then drain. Melt the coconut oil in a pan, then add the mustard seeds and curry leaves and cook until sizzling. Remove from the heat and allow to cool slightly. Put the lentils, flour, chilli, onion, spices, desiccated coconut, lime juice and 1 tsp salt in a bowl. Mix with your hands until combined, then add the coconut oil and aromatics and mix to a dough. Form into 12 dumplings, then put on top of the stew, cover with a lid and cook on low for 5 mins. Top with pepper, coriander and spring onion to serve.

Roasted cauli-broc bowl with tahini hummus

Prep: 10 mins **Cook:** 30 mins

Serves 2

Ingredients

- 400g pack cauliflower & broccoli florets
- 2 tbsp olive oil
- 250g ready-to-eat quinoa
- 2 cooked beetroots, sliced
- large handful baby spinach
- 10 walnuts, toasted and chopped
- 2 tbsp tahini
- 3 tbsp hummus
- 1 lemon, 1/2 juiced, 1/2 cut into wedges

Method

STEP 1

The night before, heat oven to 200C/180C fan/gas 6. Put the cauliflower and broccoli in a large roasting tin with the oil and a sprinkle of flaky sea salt. Roast for 25-30 mins until browned and cooked. Leave to cool completely.

STEP 2

Build each bowl by putting half the quinoa in each. Lay the slices of beetroot on top, followed by the spinach, cauliflower, broccoli and walnuts. Combine the tahini, hummus, lemon juice and 1 tbsp water in a small pot. Before eating, coat in the dressing. Serve with the lemon wedges.

Griddled vegetables with melting aubergines

Prep: 10 mins **Cook:** 25 mins

Serves 2

Ingredients

- 1 large aubergine
- ½ a lemon, zested and juiced
- 3 cloves of garlic, 1 crushed, 2 chopped
- 2 tbsp chopped parsley, plus extra to serve
- 1 tsp extra virgin olive oil, plus a little for drizzling
- 4 tsp omega seed mix (see tip)
- 2 tsp thyme leaves
- 1 tbsp rapeseed oil
- 1 red pepper, deseeded and cut into quarters
- 1 large onion, thickly sliced
- 2 courgettes, sliced on the angle
- 2 large tomatoes, each cut into 3 thick slices
- 8 Kalamata olives, halved

Method

STEP 1

Grill the aubergine, turning frequently, until soft all over and the skin is blistered, about 8-10 mins. Alternatively, if you have a gas hob, cook it directly over the flame. When it is cool enough to handle, remove the skin, finely chop the flesh and mix with the lemon juice, 1 chopped clove garlic, 1 tbsp parsley, 1 tsp extra virgin olive oil and the seeds. Mix the remaining parsley with the remaining chopped garlic and the lemon zest.

STEP 2

Meanwhile, mix the thyme, crushed garlic and rapeseed oil and toss with the vegetables, keeping the onions as slices rather than breaking up into rings. Heat a large griddle pan and char the vegetables until tender and marked with lines – the tomatoes will need the least time. Pile onto plates with the aubergine purée and olives, drizzle over a little extra olive oil and scatter with the parsley, lemon zest and garlic.

Kung pao-style cauliflower & kidney beans

Prep: 15 mins **Cook:** 25 mins

Serves 2

Ingredients

- ½ tbsp Sichuan peppercorns
- 3 tbsp vegetable oil or groundnut oil
- 1 small cauliflower (400g-500g prepped weight), broken up into large florets and stalk cut into 2cm pieces.
- 1 tbsp cornflour
- 3 garlic cloves, finely chopped
- thumb-sized piece ginger, finely chopped
- 1 tbsp chilli flakes (or to taste)
- 1 bunch spring onions, finely sliced on the the diagonal
- 2 tbsp maple syrup
- 5 tbsp light soy sauce
- 1 ½ tbsp rice vinegar or balsamic vinegar
- 400g can kidney beans, drained and rinsed
- small bunch of coriander, roughly chopped (optional)
- large handful of salted peanuts, roughly chopped

Method

STEP 1

Put the peppercorns in a dry frying pan and toast over a medium heat for 3 mins, stirring frequently. Tip onto a plate.

STEP 2

Put 2 tbsp oil in the frying pan, add the cauliflower and cook over a high heat for 5 mins to colour. Meanwhile, blitz the peppercorns in a small food processor or grind using a pestle and mortar and mix with the cornflour.

STEP 3

Drizzle the remaining 1 tbsp oil in the pan and add a third of the cornflour mix to coat the cauliflower. Cook for 1 min, then add the garlic, ginger, chilli, three-quarters of the spring onions and 400ml water.

STEP 4

Cover with a lid or baking tray and boil for a couple of mins. As this cooks, add the maple syrup, soy sauce and vinegar, plus 6 tbsp water, to the remaining cornflour mix in a separate bowl. Stir until smooth and set aside.

STEP 5

Add the maple cornflour mix to the cauliflower, stirring. Bring to the boil, then turn down the heat, add the beans, cover and simmer until the sauce thickens and the cauliflower is tender.

STEP 6

Tip onto a plate, scatter over the coriander, if using, then top with the remaining spring onions and the peanuts.

Fluffy almond pancakes with blueberry ripple yogurt

Prep: 10 mins **Cook:** 20 mins

Serves 6

Ingredients

- 300g self raising flour
- 1 tsp baking powder
- 1 tbsp vanilla extract
- 400-450ml Alpro almond drink, unsweetened
- 1 tbsp vegetable oil, for cooking

For the blueberry ripple yogurt

- 250g blueberries
- 400g Alpro Simply plain yogurt alternative

Method

STEP 1

Put the blueberries in a small pan with 1 tbsp water and simmer over a low heat for 5-8 mins until the berries burst. Increase the heat a little and cook for another 3-4 mins until it's a jam-like consistency, then transfer to a bowl and leave to cool.

STEP 2

Stir the flour and baking powder together in a large bowl with a big pinch of salt, then whisk in the vanilla and almond milk until it forms a smooth, thick batter.

STEP 3

Heat a little of the oil in a non-stick pan and spoon ½ a ladleful of the pancake mix into the pan. Fry for 4 mins until the edges are set, then flip and fry for another 2-3 mins until both sides are golden. Repeat with a little more oil and batter, until all the pancakes are cooked and you have 12 small-medium sized pancakes. Keep warm in a low oven while you cook the remaining batter, if you like.

STEP 4

Briefly fold half of the blueberry compote through the yogurt to give it a ripple effect. Layer the pancakes with the remaining compote, then add a generous dollop of yogurt to serve.

Luxury hummus

Prep: 20 mins **Cook:** 5 mins

Serves 8

Ingredients

- 700g chickpeas , drained
- 135ml extra virgin olive oil , plus extra for drizzling
- 2 garlic cloves , roughly chopped
- 1 tbsp tahini
- 1 ½ lemons , juiced

For the toppings

- ½ tsp smoked paprika
- ½ tsp sumac
- ½ small pack parsley , roughly chopped
- 40g pomegranate seeds

crudités and warm pittas, to serve

Method

STEP 1

Blitz ¾ of the chickpeas and 120ml of the oil with the rest of the hummus ingredients and a good amount of seasoning in a food processor. Add a little water if it is too thick. Spoon the hummus into a serving bowl or spread it onto a plate. Can be made up to two days in advance and kept in the fridge.

STEP 2

Dry the rest of the chickpeas on kitchen paper as much as possible. Heat the remaining oil in a frying pan over a medium heat. Add the chickpeas and a large pinch of salt, and fry until golden, around 4 mins. Drain on kitchen paper.

STEP 3

Drizzle some oil over the hummus, then sprinkle with the spices, parsley and pomegranate seeds. Scatter the fried chickpeas on top and serve with crudités and warm pitta breads.

Roasted root veg traybake

Prep: 15 mins **Cook:** 50 mins

Serves 4

Ingredients

- 1kg mixed roots – we used carrots, parsnips and swede – cut into batons and halved
- 220g new potatoes , halved
- 3 garlic cloves , skin left on
- 4 rosemary sprigs
- 4 thyme sprigs
- 2 tbsp olive oil
- 50g pack mixed snacking nuts or seeds
- 45g vegetarian feta

For the roasted garlic & herb dressing

- 2 tbsp olive oil
- 1 small pack parsley , finely chopped
- 1 lemon , juiced

Method

STEP 1

Heat oven to 200C/180C fan/gas 5. Tip the roots, potatoes and garlic cloves into a large roasting tin. Nestle the herbs in amongst them, then drizzle with olive oil and toss, so everything is well coated. Season and roast for 50 mins, or until all the vegetables are tender.

STEP 2

Squeeze the roasted garlic out of its skin and blitz with the rest of the dressing ingredients. Alternatively, you can whisk these together in a small bowl. Toss the roots in the dressing, scatter over the nuts, feta and serve.

Staffordshire oatcakes with mushrooms

Prep: 15 mins **Cook:** 20 mins

plus at least 2 hrs proving

Serves 4

Ingredients

For the oatcakes

- 85g porridge oats
- 85g plain wholemeal flour
- ½ tsp dried yeast

For the topping

- 4 tsp rapeseed oil , plus a little for frying
- 320g button mushrooms , sliced
- 4 tomatoes , each cut into 8 wedges
- 4 tbsp milled seeds with flax and chia
- 4 tbsp tahini
- a few coriander sprigs, chopped

Method

STEP 1

For the oatcakes, tip the oats and 350ml water into a bowl and blitz with a stick blender until smooth (alternatively you can use a food processor or liquidizer). Stir in the flour and yeast, cover and leave in the fridge overnight, or leave at room temperature for 2-3 hrs until bubbles appear.

STEP 2

Use kitchen paper to rub ½ tsp oil round a non-stick frying pan, then heat. Ladle in a quarter of the batter and swirl the pan to cover the base (the oatcakes should be a few millimeters thick, like a crêpe). Cook for 2 mins, then turn and cook for 2 mins more until golden. Make four oatcakes in the same way. If you're following our Healthy Diet Plan, chill two for another day. Will keep, covered in the fridge, for two days.

STEP 3

To make the topping for two oatcakes, heat 2 tsp oil in a non-stick pan, add 160g mushrooms and fry for 2-3 mins, stirring until softened. Stir in 2 tomatoes, then add 2 tbsp ground seeds and cook for 2 mins more. Reheat the oatcakes in a dry frying pan or the microwave if necessary, then spread each one with 1 tbsp tahini, the mushroom mixture and scatter with a little coriander before serving. On the second day, repeat step 3 with the remaining ingredients.

Rhubarb gin

Prep: 10 mins

plus 4 weeks infusing, no cook

makes 2 litres

Ingredients

- 1kg pink rhubarb stalks
- 400g caster sugar (don't use golden - it muddies the colour)
- 800ml gin

Method

STEP 1

Wash the rhubarb, trim the stalks and discard the base and any leaves. Cut the stalks into 3cm lengths. Put in a large jar with the sugar. Shake everything around, put the lid on and leave overnight. The sugar will draw the juice out of the rhubarb.

STEP 2

After 24 hrs, add the gin, seal and shake everything around. Leave for about 4 weeks before drinking. You can strain the liquor off through a muslin-lined sieve and transfer to a bottle, but I often just leave the rhubarb and booze in the jar and ladle it into drinks that way. Over time the rhubarb and the gin go a much paler colour – this doesn't look as dramatic. The upside is you that have to get through it fairly quickly!

Miso aubergines

Prep: 5 mins **Cook:** 50 mins

Serves 2

Ingredients

- 2 small aubergines, halved
- vegetable oil, for roasting and frying
- 50g brown miso
- 100g giant couscous
- 1 red chilli, thinly sliced
- ½ small pack coriander, leaves chopped

Method

STEP 1

Heat oven to 180C/160C fan/ gas 4. With a sharp knife, criss-cross the flesh of the aubergines in a diagonal pattern, then place on a baking tray. Brush the flesh with 1 tbsp vegetable oil.

STEP 2

Mix the miso with 25ml water to make a thick paste. Spread the paste over the aubergines, then cover the tray with foil and roast in the centre of the oven for 30 mins.

STEP 3

Remove the foil and roast the aubergines for a further 15-20 mins, depending on their size, until tender.

STEP 4

Meanwhile, bring a saucepan of salted water to the boil and heat 1 /2 tbsp vegetable oil over a medium-high heat in a frying pan. Add the couscous to the frying pan, toast for 2 mins until golden brown, then tip into the pan of boiling water and cook for 8-10 mins until tender (or following pack instructions). Drain well. Serve the aubergines with the couscous, topped with the chilli and a scattering of coriander leaves.

Veggie olive wraps with mustard vinaigrette

Prep: 10 mins

Serves 1

Ingredients

- 1 carrot , shredded or coarsely grated
- 80g wedge red cabbage , finely shredded
- 2 spring onions , thinly sliced
- 1 courgette , shredded or coarsely grated
- handful basil leaves
- 5 green olives , pitted and halved
- ½ tsp English mustard powder
- 2 tsp extra virgin rapeseed oil
- 1 tbsp cider vinegar
- 1 large seeded tortilla

Method

STEP 1

Mix all the ingredients except for the tortilla and toss well.

STEP 2

Put the tortilla on a sheet of foil and pile the filling along one side of the wrap – it will almost look like too much mixture, but once you start to roll it firmly it will compact. Roll the tortilla from the filling side, folding in the sides as you go. Fold the foil in at the ends to keep stuff inside the wrap. Cut in half and eat straight away. If taking to work, leave whole and wrap up like a cracker in baking parchment.

Basic lentils

Prep: 10 mins **Cook:** 45 mins

Makes 6 portions

Ingredients

- 2 tbsp coconut oil
- 2 onions , chopped
- 4 garlic cloves , chopped
- large piece of ginger , chopped
- 300g red split lentils
- 1 tsp turmeric
- 2 tomatoes , roughly chopped
- 1 tsp coriander seeds
- 1 tsp cumin seeds
- 1 tsp black mustard seeds
- 1 lemon , juiced

Method

STEP 1

Melt 1 tbsp coconut oil in a large saucepan. Add the onion and a pinch of salt, and cook for 8 mins. Stir in the garlic and ginger and cook for a few mins more. Add the lentils, turmeric and tomatoes, stir to combine, then pour in 1 litre of water. Bring to the boil, then turn down and simmer for 25-30 mins, stirring occasionally, until the lentils are tender.

STEP 2

Heat the rest of the oil in a frying pan. When it's very hot, add the spices and fry for a min or so until fragrant, then stir them through. Add the lemon juice and season to taste. Will keep for four days in the fridge, or freeze it in batches and use to make our lentil kedgeree, lentil fritters, or spinach dhal with harissa yogurt.

Seitan & black bean stir-fry

Prep: 20 mins **Cook:** 25 mins

Serves 4

Ingredients

For the sauce

- 400g can black beans, drained and rinsed
- 75g dark brown soft sugar
- 3 garlic cloves
- 2 tbsp soy sauce
- 1 tsp Chinese five-spice powder
- 2 tbsp rice vinegar
- 1 tbsp smooth peanut butter
- 1 red chilli, finely chopped

For the stir-fry

- 350g jar marinated seitan pieces (we used Biona)
- 1 tbsp cornflour
- 2-3 tbsp vegetable oil
- 1 red pepper, sliced
- 300g pak choi, chopped
- 2 spring onions, sliced
- cooked rice noodles or rice, to serve

Method

STEP 1

Start by making the sauce, tip half the beans into the bowl of a food processor with the rest of the ingredients and add 50ml water. Season, then blend until smooth. Pour into a saucepan and heat gently for about 5 mins or until thick and glossy.

STEP 2

Drain the seitan and pat dry with kitchen paper. Toss the seitan pieces in a bowl with the cornflour and set aside. Heat your wok to a high temperature, add a little oil, then the seitan – you might need to do this in batches. Stir-fry for around 5 mins until golden brown at the edges. Remove the seitan from the wok using a slotted spoon and set aside on a plate.

STEP 3

If the wok is dry at this stage, add 1 tsp vegetable oil. Add the shallots and stir-fry until soft. Throw in the chopped peppers, the rest of the beans, pak choi and spring onion. Cook for 3-4 mins, then return the seitan to the pan, stir in the sauce and bring to the boil for 1 min. Serve with cooked rice or noodles.

Chapatis

Prep: 15 mins **Cook:** 10 mins

Makes 10

Ingredients

- 140g wholemeal flour
- 140g plain flour, plus extra for dusting
- 1 tsp salt
- 2 tbsp olive oil, plus extra for greasing
- 180ml hot water or as needed

Method

STEP 1

In a large bowl, stir together the flours and salt. Use a wooden spoon to stir in the olive oil and enough water to make a soft dough that is elastic but not sticky.

STEP 2

Knead the dough on a lightly floured surface for 5-10 mins until it is smooth. Divide into 10 pieces, or less if you want bigger breads. Roll each piece into a ball. Let rest for a few mins.

STEP 3

Heat a frying pan over medium heat until hot, and grease lightly. On a lightly floured surface, use a floured rolling pin to roll out the balls of dough until very thin like a tortilla.

STEP 4

When the pan starts smoking, put a chapati on it. Cook until the underside has brown spots, about 30 seconds, then flip and cook on the other side. Put on a plate and keep warm while you cook the rest of the chapatis.

Tarka dhal

Prep: 10 mins **Cook:** 1 hr

Serves 2

Ingredients

- 200g red lentils
- 2 tbsp ghee , or vegetable oil if you're vegan
- 1 small onion , finely chopped
- 3 garlic cloves , finely chopped
- ¼ tsp turmeric
- ½ tsp garam masala
- coriander , to serve
- 1 small tomato , chopped

Method

STEP 1

Rinse the lentils several times until the water runs clear, then tip into a saucepan with 1 litre water and a pinch of salt. Bring to the boil, then reduce the heat and simmer for 25 mins, skimming the froth from the top. Cover with a lid and cook for a further 40 mins, stirring occasionally, until it's a thick, soupy consistency.

STEP 2

While the lentils are cooking, heat the ghee or oil in a non-stick frying pan over a medium heat, then fry the onion and garlic until the onion is softened, so around 8 mins. Add the turmeric and garam masala, then cook for a further minute. Set aside.

STEP 3

Tip the lentils into bowls and spoon half the onion mixture on top. Top with the coriander and tomato to serve.

Saag aloo

Prep: 10 mins **Cook:** 15 mins

Serves 4 as a side dish

Ingredients

- 2 tbsp sunflower oil
- 1 onion, finely chopped
- 2 garlic cloves, sliced
- 1 tbsp chopped ginger
- 500g potato, cut into 2cm (¾in) chunks
- 1 large red chilli, halved, deseeded and finely sliced
- ½ tsp each black mustard seeds, cumin seeds, turmeric
- 250g spinach leaves

Method

STEP 1

Heat 2 tbsp sunflower oil in a large pan, add 1 finely chopped onion, 2 sliced garlic cloves and 1 tbsp chopped ginger, and fry for about 3 mins.

STEP 2

Stir in 500g potatoes, cut into 2cm chunks, 1 halved, deseeded and finely sliced red chilli, ½ tsp black mustard seeds, ½ tsp cumin seeds, ½ tsp turmeric and ½ tsp salt and continue cooking and stirring for 5 mins more.

STEP 3

Add a splash of water, cover, and cook for 8-10 mins.

STEP 4

Check the potatoes are ready by spearing with the point of a knife, and if they are, add 250g spinach leaves and let it wilt into the pan. Take off the heat and serve.

Tomato bruschetta

Prep: 15 mins **Cook:** 5 mins

Makes 12

Ingredients

- ½ small red onion, finely chopped

- 8 medium tomatoes (about 500g), coarsely chopped and drained
- 2-3 garlic cloves, crushed
- 6-8 leaves of fresh basil, finely chopped
- 30ml balsamic vinegar
- 60-80ml extra virgin olive oil
- 1 loaf crusty bread

Method

STEP 1

In a large bowl, mix the onions, tomatoes, garlic and basil, taking care not to mash or break up the tomatoes too much. Add the balsamic vinegar and extra virgin olive oil. Add salt and pepper to taste. Mix again. Cover and chill for at least an hour. This will allow the flavours to soak and blend together.

STEP 2

Slice the baguette loaf diagonally into 12 thick slices and lightly toast them until they are light brown on both sides. Serve the mixture on the warm slices of bread. If you prefer the mixture at room temperature, remove from the fridge half an hour before serving.

Avocado hummus & crudités

Prep: 10 mins

Serves 2

Ingredients

- 1 avocado, peeled and stoned
- 210g chickpeas, drained
- 1 garlic clove, crushed
- pinch chilli flakes, plus extra to serve
- 1 lime, juiced
- handful coriander leaves
- 2 carrots, cut into strips
- 2 mixed peppers, cut into strips
- 160g sugar snap peas

Method

STEP 1

Blitz together the avocado, chickpeas, garlic, chilli flakes and lime juice, and season to taste. Top the hummus with the coriander leaves and a few more chilli flakes, and serve with the carrot, pepper and sugar snap crudités. Make the night before for a great take-to-work lunch.

Garlicky mushroom penne

Prep: 20 mins **Cook:** 15 mins

Serves 2

Ingredients

- 210g can chickpeas , no need to drain
- 1 tbsp lemon juice
- 1 large garlic clove
- 1 tsp vegetable bouillon
- 2 tsp tahini
- ¼ tsp ground coriander
- 115g wholemeal penne
- 2 tsp rapeseed oil
- 2 red onions , halved and sliced
- 200g closed cup mushrooms , roughly chopped
- ½ lemon , juiced
- generous handful chopped parsley

Method

STEP 1

To make the hummus, tip a 210g can chickpeas with the liquid into a bowl and add 1 tbsp lemon juice, 1 large garlic clove, 1 tsp vegetable bouillon, 2 tsp tahini and ¼ tsp ground coriander.

STEP 2

Blitz to a wet paste with a hand blender, still retaining some texture from the chickpeas.

STEP 3

Cook 115g wholemeal penne pasta according to the pack instructions.

STEP 4

Meanwhile, heat 2 tsp rapeseed oil in a non-stick wok or large frying pan and add 2 halved and sliced red onions and 200g roughly chopped closed cup mushrooms, stirring frequently until softened and starting to caramelise.

STEP 5

Toss together lightly, squeeze over the juice of ½ a lemon and serve, adding a dash of water to loosen the mixture a little if needed. Scatter with a generous handful of chopped parsley.

Vegetarian Thai green curry

Prep: 15 mins **Cook:** 40 mins

Serves 4

Ingredients

- 2 tbsp vegetable oil
- 3 shallots, finely sliced
- 4 tbsp Thai green curry paste
- 1 red chilli, deseeded and finely chopped
- 350g butternut squash, peeled and cut into 1.5cm cubes
- 1 large red pepper, deseeded and cut into thick slices
- 400g can full fat coconut milk
- 5 dried kaffir lime leaves
- 150g mangetout
- 100g baby corn. halved lengthways
- 1 small bunch coriander, roughly chopped

- cooked rice and lime wedges, to serve

Method

STEP 1

Heat the oil in a large flameproof casserole dish with a tight-fitting lid. Add the shallots with a generous pinch of salt and fry for 7-10 mins over a medium heat until softened and beginning to caramelise. Add the curry paste and chilli to the dish and fry for 2 mins. Tip in the squash and pepper, then stir through the coconut milk along with 200ml water. Add the lime leaves, cover and cook for 15-20 mins or until the squash is tender.

STEP 2

Stir the mangetout and baby corn through the curry, then re-cover, cooking over a medium-low heat for a further 5 mins or until the veg is just cooked. Season and stir through half the coriander. Remove the lime leaves and discard. Spoon the curry into deep bowls, scatter with the remaining coriander and serve with rice and lime wedges for squeezing over.

Chilli-charred Brussels sprouts

Prep: 15 mins **Cook:** 25 mins

Serves 6

Ingredients

- 600g Brussels sprouts , trimmed at the base
- 60ml olive oil
- 4 garlic cloves , peeled and bashed
- 1-2 tsp chilli flakes
- 1 lemon , zested and juiced

Method

STEP 1

Bring a pan of salted water to the boil. Add the Brussels sprouts and cook for 4-5 mins until just tender, then drain and leave to cool a little before slicing in half vertically.

STEP 2

Meanwhile, heat 3 tbsp olive oil in a large frying pan over a medium heat, add the garlic and cook until golden but not burnt, around 4 mins. Use a slotted spoon to remove the garlic and discard. Add the chilli flakes and a big pinch of salt to the oil, then put the sprouts cut-side down in the pan, and leave them to cook for around 10 mins. Don't be tempted to move them – this ensures that they get some colour. Add the remaining olive oil and the lemon juice, then cook for a few mins more.

STEP 3

Tip onto a large serving platter, top with lemon zest and season. These will hold in a low oven for 20 mins while you get everything else ready.

Lentil ragu with courgetti

Prep: 15 mins **Cook:** 40 mins

Serves 4 - 6

Ingredients

- 2 tbsp rapeseed oil , plus 1 tsp
- 3 celery sticks , chopped
- 2 carrots , chopped
- 4 garlic cloves , chopped
- 2 onions , finely chopped
- 140g button mushrooms from a 280g pack, quartered
- 500g pack dried red lentils
- 500g pack passata
- 1l reduced-salt vegetable bouillon (we used Marigold)
- 1 tsp dried oregano
- 2 tbsp balsamic vinegar
- 1-2 large courgettes , cut into noodles with a spiraliser, julienne peeler or knife

Method

STEP 1

Heat the 2 tbsp oil in a large sauté pan. Add the celery, carrots, garlic and onions, and fry for 4-5 mins over a high heat to soften and start to colour. Add the mushrooms and fry for 2 mins more.

STEP 2

Stir in the lentils, passata, bouillon, oregano and balsamic vinegar. Cover the pan and leave to simmer for 30 mins until the lentils are tender and pulpy. Check occasionally and stir to make sure the mixture isn't sticking to the bottom of the pan; if it does, add a drop of water.

STEP 3

To serve, heat the remaining oil in a separate frying pan, add the courgette and stir-fry briefly to soften and warm through. Serve half the ragu with the courgetti and chill the rest to eat on another day. Can be frozen for up to 3 months.

Turmeric latte

Prep: 5 mins **Cook:** 5 mins

Serves 2

Ingredients

- 350ml almond milk (or any milk of your choice)
- ¼ tsp ground turmeric
- ¼ tsp ground cinnamon
- ¼ tsp ground ginger
- ½ tsp vanilla extract
- 1 tsp maple syrup
- grind of black pepper

Method

STEP 1

Put all the ingredients in a saucepan and whisk constantly over a gentle heat, ideally with a milk frother if you have one. Once hot, pour into mugs and sprinkle with a little more cinnamon to serve.

Squash & cabbage sabzi

Prep: 10 mins **Cook:** 10 mins

Serves 2 as a main or 4 as a side

Ingredients

- 2 tbsp sunflower oil
- 1 tsp nigella seeds
- thumb-sized piece ginger , grated
- 2 garlic cloves , grated

- 200g pumpkin or butternut squash, peeled and chopped into 1-2cm cubes
- 200g cabbage , chopped (sweetheart or pointed cabbage works well)
- 1 tsp turmeric
- 1 tsp ground coriander
- 1 tsp ground cumin
- 1 tsp chilli flakes
- 2 tsp lime juice
- dhal , chutney and rice or roti to serve (optional)

Method

STEP 1

Heat the oil in a frying pan and add the nigella seeds. When they start popping, add the ginger and garlic, and cook for 1 min. Add the squash, cabbage, spices and 1 tsp salt, then mix everything together well with a splash of water, covering the pan with a lid. Leave to steam for 7-8 mins over a low heat.

STEP 2

After this time, lift the lid to check if the squash is cooked. If not, replace the lid quickly and leave to cook a little longer. Add the lime juice and check for seasoning before serving with dhal, chutney and rice or roti, if you like.

Kentucky fried seitan

Prep:45 mins **Cook:**50 mins

Serves 4 - 6

Ingredients

- 250g firm tofu
- 150ml unsweetened soy milk
- 2 tsp miso paste
- 2 tsp Marmite
- 1 tsp dried tarragon
- 1 tsp dried sage
- 1 tsp dried thyme

- 1 tsp onion powder
- 2 tsp garlic powder
- 160g wheat gluten
- 40g pea protein or vegan protein powder
- 1.5 litres vegetable stock
- 1 onion , quartered
- 3 garlic cloves
- handful parsley stalks
- 300g gram flour
- 350g plain flour
- vegetable or sunflower oil for frying

For the spice coating

- 2 tsp dried thyme
- 2 tsp dried basil
- 2 tsp dried oregano
- 2 tsp ground ginger
- 3 tsp celery salt
- 3 tsp black pepper
- 3 tsp white pepper
- 3 tsp dried mustard
- 3 tsp paprika
- 3 tsp dried sage
- 4 tsp dried garlic powder
- 1 tsp brown sugar
- 200g panko breadcrumbs

Method

STEP 1

First, make the seitan. Blitz the tofu, soy milk, miso, marmite, tarragon, sage, thyme, onion powder, garlic powder, 1 tsp salt and ½ tsp white pepper in a food processor until smooth.

STEP 2

Tip into a bowl and add the wheat gluten and pea protein or protein powder. Mix to form a dough. Once it has come together, give it a really good knead, stretching and tearing for 10-15 mins. It will be ready when the seitan feels springy.

STEP 3

Pour the veg stock into a pan with the onion, garlic and parsley stalks. Bring to a simmer. Flatten out the seitan to 1cm in thickness, and chop into chicken-breast-sized chunks. Simmer these in the stock for 30 mins, covered with a lid. Allow to cool in the stock. Ideally do this the day before and chill in the fridge. These can also be frozen if you wish.

STEP 4

Mix the spice coating ingredients in one bowl. Place the gram flour in another and the plain flour in a third. Mix enough water into the gram flour until it has a texture similar to beaten egg. Dip the seitan pieces in the plain flour, shake off the excess, then coat each piece in the gram flour mixture and finally in the panko spice mix.

STEP 5

In a large frying pan or deep fat fryer, heat the oil to 180C (or until a piece of bread browns in 20 seconds). Once it's hot, carefully drop in the seitan pieces and cook for 6 mins or so, until they are dark golden brown and crispy. Transfer to kitchen paper to drain off the excess oil and sprinkle with a little salt. Serve in toasted buns with salad or slaw, or alternatively as mock chicken dippers with BBQ sauce.

Spiced aubergine bake

Prep: 15 mins **Cook:** 45 mins - 55 mins

Serves 4 - 6

Ingredients

- 4 aubergines, cut into 5mm-1cm slices
- 3 tbsp vegetable oil
- 2 tbsp coconut oil
- 2 large onions, chopped
- 3 garlic cloves, crushed
- 1 tbsp black mustard seeds

- ½ tbsp fenugreek seeds
- 1 tbsp garam masala
- ¼ tsp hot chilli powder
- 1 cinnamon stick
- 1 tsp ground cumin
- 1 tsp ground coriander
- 2 x 400g cans chopped tomatoes
- 200ml coconut milk
- sugar, to taste
- 2 tbsp flaked almonds
- small bunch coriander, roughly chopped (optional)

Method

STEP 1

Heat oven to 220C/200C fan/gas 7. Generously brush each aubergine slice with vegetable oil and place in a single layer on a baking tray, or two if they don't fit on one. Cook on the low shelves for 10 mins, then turn over and cook for a further 5-10 mins until they are golden. Reduce the oven to 180C/160C fan/gas 4.

STEP 2

Heat the coconut oil in a large, heavy-based frying pan and add the onions. Cover and sweat on a low heat for about 5 mins until softened. Add the garlic, mustard seeds, fenugreek seeds, garam masala, chilli powder, cinnamon stick, cumin and ground coriander. Cook for a few secs until it starts to smell beautiful and aromatic.

STEP 3

Pour the chopped tomatoes and coconut milk into the spiced onions and stir well. Check the seasoning and add a little sugar, salt or pepper to taste.

STEP 4

Spoon a third of the tomato sauce on the bottom of a 2-litre ovenproof dish. Layer with half the aubergine slices. Spoon over a further third of tomato sauce, then the remaining aubergine slices, and finish with the rest of the sauce. Sprinkle over the flaked almonds and coriander (if using), reserving some to serve, and bake for 25-30 mins. Serve garnished with more coriander.

Spring tabbouleh

Prep: 20 mins **Cook:** 25 mins

Serves 4

Ingredients

- 6 tbsp olive oil
- 1 tbsp garam masala
- 2 x 400g cans chickpeas, drained and rinsed
- 250g ready-to-eat mixed grain pouch
- 250g frozen peas
- 2 lemons, zested and juiced
- large pack parsley, leaves roughly chopped
- large pack mint, leaves roughly chopped
- 250g radishes, roughly chopped
- 1 cucumber, chopped

- pomegranate seeds, to serve

Method

STEP 1

Heat oven to 200C/180C fan/ gas 6. Mix 4 tbsp oil with the garam masala and some seasoning. Toss with the chickpeas in a large roasting tin, then cook for 15 mins until starting to crisp. Tip in the mixed grains, peas and lemon zest. Mix well, then return to the oven for about 10 mins until warmed through.

STEP 2

Transfer to a large bowl or platter, then toss through the herbs, radishes, cucumber, remaining oil and lemon juice. Season to taste and scatter over the pomegranate seeds. Any leftovers will be good for lunch the next day.

Hummus

Prep: 10 mins

Serves 4

Ingredients

- 400g can chickpeas, drained
- 80ml extra virgin olive oil
- 1-2 fat garlic cloves, peeled and crushed
- 1 lemon, juiced then ½ zested
- 3 tbsp tahini

mixed crudités and toasted pitta bread, to serve (optional)

Method

STEP 1

Thoroughly rinse the chickpeas in a colander under cold running water. Tip into the large bowl of a food processor along with 60ml of the oil and blitz until almost smooth. Add the garlic, lemon and tahini along with 30ml water. Blitz again for about 5 mins, or until the hummus is smooth and silky.

STEP 2

Add 20ml more water, a little at a time, if it looks too thick. Season and transfer to a bowl. Swirl the top of the hummus with the back of a dessert spoon and drizzle over the remaining oil. Serve with crunchy crudités and toasted pitta bread, if you like.

Beetroot, hummus & crispy chickpea sub sandwich

Prep: 10 mins **Cook:** 10 mins

Serves 2

Ingredients

- 300g pack cooked beetroot in water, drained, half sliced
- 400g can chickpeas , drained
- 3 tbsp vegan pesto
- olive oil
- splash of vinegar (white wine vinegar if you have it)
- 2 large ciabatta rolls, sliced in half

- 2 large handfuls mixed rocket, watercress & spinach salad

Method

STEP 1

Blitz the whole beetroot, ¾ of the chickpeas, 2 tbsp pesto and 1 tbsp oil in a food processor with some seasoning until you have a thick, smooth hummus. Heat the ciabatta following the pack instructions.

STEP 2

Fry the remaining chickpeas in a little oil until crisp, then set aside. Toss the salad leaves with the remaining pesto and a splash of vinegar. Slice the rolls, then assemble the sandwiches with the hummus, beetroot slices, salad leaves and fried chickpeas.

Chocolate & date tart

Prep: 30 mins **Cook:** 40 mins

Serves 8

- **Ingredients**
- flour, for rolling
- 320g shortcrust pastry sheet (we used Jus-Rol, which is vegan)
- 180g medjool dates, pitted and chopped
- 400ml coconut milk
- 1 tsp vanilla extract
- 200g dairy-free dark chocolate, finely chopped
- 3 tbsp coconut oil
- 1 tbsp cocoa powder
- ½ tbsp icing sugar

Method

STEP 1

Un-roll the pastry sheet onto a lightly floured surface, mix the cocoa powder and icing sugar together. Use a sieve to sprinkle all over the pastry sheet, then fold in half like a book and chill for 15 mins. On a lightly floured surface, roll the pastry sheet into a slightly larger rectangle, big enough to line a 20cm tart tin. Line the tin, leaving any overhanging pastry – you'll trim this away once the tart is baked. Chill for 30 mins on a baking tray. Heat oven to 200C/180C fan/gas 6.

STEP 2

Line the pastry with greaseproof paper and fill with baking beans. Bake for 15-20 mins, then remove the paper and beans and bake for 15 mins more, until cooked through. Remove from the oven and leave the case to cool in its tin, then trim the sides.

STEP 3

While the pastry is cooling, make the date caramel. Warm the coconut milk until steaming, then pour 120ml of the coconut milk over the dates. Soak for 5 mins then tip into a food processor with the vanilla extract and a big pinch of flaky salt. Blitz until smooth. Spread the caramel onto the base of the tart and put in the fridge for 30 mins to set a little.

STEP 4

To make the ganache topping, heat the remaining coconut milk over a low heat until steaming. Put the chocolate and coconut oil in a large bowl and pour the warm coconut milk over the top. Leave to sit for a minute, then gently stir until combined. Spoon the mixture over the caramel and spread it out – don't worry if the caramel comes up the sides a bit. Sprinkle with flaky sea salt and leave to set in the fridge for about an hour, then bring to room temperature before slicing and serving.

Squash & spinach fusilli with pecans

Prep: 10 mins **Cook:** 40 mins

Serves 2

Ingredients

- 160g butternut squash , diced
- 3 garlic cloves , sliced
- 1 tbsp chopped sage leaves
- 2 tsp rapeseed oil
- 1 large courgette , halved and sliced
- 6 pecan halves
- 115g wholemeal fusilli

- 125g bag baby spinach

Method

STEP 1

Heat oven to 200C/180C fan/gas 6. Toss the butternut squash, garlic and sage in the oil, then spread out in a roasting tin and cook in the oven for 20 mins, add the courgettes and cook for a further 15 mins. Give everything a stir, then add the pecans and cook for 5 mins more until the nuts are toasted and the vegetables are tender and starting to caramelise.

STEP 2

Meanwhile, boil the pasta according to pack instructions – about 12 mins. Drain, then tip into a serving bowl and toss with the spinach so that it wilts in the heat from the pasta. Add the roasted veg and pecans, breaking up the nuts a little, and toss again really well before serving.

Curried cashew dip

Prep: 5 mins

Serves 4

Ingredients

- 100g cashew nuts
- 1-2 limes , juiced (apron 50ml)
- 3 tbsp coconut cream
- 2 tbsp korma curry paste
- 2 tbsp Bombay spice mix

To serve

- chicken skewers, carrot sticks and naan bread

Method

STEP 1

Tip all the ingredients, except the Bombay mix, into a food processor. Blend until smooth, then season to taste. If the mixture is too thick, add a little more lime juice or a splash of cold water.

STEP 2

Spoon into a bowl and sprinkle over the Bombay mix before serving with chicken skewers, carrot sticks and naan bread.

Spiced roast cauliflower with herby rice

Prep: 10 mins **Cook:** 30 mins

Serves 2

Ingredients

- 1 cauliflower , broken into florets
- 2 red peppers , cut into chunky pieces
- 1 red onion , 1/2 quartered, 1/2 sliced
- 3 tbsp olive oil
- 1 tbsp ras el hanout
- 1 garlic clove , crushed
- 200ml vegan coconut yogurt (such as Coconut Collaborative or COYO)
- 125g basmati rice
- 400ml vegan vegetable stock (such as Marigold Vegan Bouillon Powder)
- small pack coriander , chopped

pomegranate seeds , to serve

Method

STEP 1

Heat oven to 200C/180C fan/gas 6. Spread out the cauliflower, peppers and onion quarters on a very large baking tray. Drizzle with 2 tbsp olive oil and sprinkle with the ras el hanout. Toss together, season and roast for 30 mins.

STEP 2

Meanwhile, stir the garlic into the yogurt and set aside. In a medium saucepan, heat the remaining oil. Add the sliced onion, season and fry for 5 mins. Add the rice and coat well in the oil. Pour over vegetable stock so that it covers it by about 2cm. Bring to the boil, then turn down to the lowest heat and cover with a lid. Check after 5 mins and add most of the coriander. Cook for 4 mins more until al dente.

STEP 3

Remove from the heat and let it sit with the lid on for 10 mins. Serve the roasted vegetables with the rice, remaining coriander, the pomegranate seeds and the yogurt sauce to share.

Veggie protein chilli

Prep: 12 mins **Cook:** 55 mins

1 after training or 2 otherwise

Ingredients

- 1 tbsp olive oil
- ½ onion , finely chopped
- ½ red chilli , finely chopped
- 1 garlic clove , finely chopped
- 1 small sweet potato , peeled and cut into chunks
- ½ tsp cumin
- ½ tsp paprika
- ½ tsp cayenne pepper
- ½ tsp cinnamon
- 400g can mixed beans
- 400g can chopped tomatoes

- 1 lime , juiced, to serve
- cauliflower rice , to serve

Method

STEP 1

Heat the oil in a large saucepan and add the onion, chilli and garlic and cook without colouring for 1-2 mins. Tip in the sweet potato, spices and some seasoning, then pour in the beans and chopped tomatoes. Fill one of the empty cans with water and add to the pan, then bring to the boil and turn down to a simmer.

STEP 2

Cook for 45-50 mins or until the sweet potato is soft and the sauce has reduced – add some water if the sauce looks a bit thick. Stir through the lime juice, season to taste and serve with cauliflower rice.

Date butter

Prep: 4 mins

Serves 4

Ingredients

- 150g coconut oil or butter
- 80g soft pitted dates
- 1 tbsp maple syrup
- pinch of cinnamon
- pinch of salt

Method

STEP 1

In a small food processor, blend the coconut oil or butter, dates (we used medjool), maple syrup, cinnamon and salt. Chill until needed, will keep for up to a week.

Walnut & almond muesli with grated apple

Prep: 10 mins **Cook:** 2 mins

Serves 4

Ingredients

- 85g porridge oats
- 15g flaked almonds
- 15g walnut pieces
- 15g pumpkin seeds
- 1 tsp ground cinnamon
- 80g raisins
- 15g high fibre puffed wheat (we used Good Grain)
- 4 apples , no need to peel, grated
- milk , to serve

Method

STEP 1

Put the porridge oats in a saucepan and heat gently, stirring frequently until they're just starting to toast. Turn off the heat, then add all of the nuts, pumpkin seeds, and cinnamon, then stir everything together well.

STEP 2

Tip into a large bowl, stir to help it cool, then add the raisins and puffed wheat and toss together until well mixed. Tip half into a jar or airtight container and save for another day – it will keep at room temperature. Serve the rest in two bowls, grate over 2 apples and pour over some cold milk (use nut milk if you're vegan) at the table. Save the other apples for the remaining muesli.

Celeriac, hazelnut & truffle soup

Prep:20 mins **Cook:**45 mins

Serves 6

Ingredients

- 1 tbsp olive oil
- small bunch thyme
- 2 bay leaves
- 1 onion , chopped
- 1 fat garlic clove , chopped
- 1 celeriac (about 1kg), peeled and chopped
- 1 potato (about 200g), chopped
- 1l veg stock (check the label to ensure it's vegan – we used Marigold)
- 100ml soya cream
- 50g blanched hazelnuts , toasted and roughly chopped
- 1 tbsp truffle oil , plus an extra drizzle to serve

Method

STEP 1

In a large saucepan, heat the oil over a low heat. Tie the thyme sprigs and bay leaves together with a piece of string and add them to the pan with the onion and a pinch of salt. Cook for about 10 mins until softened but not coloured.

STEP 2

Stir in the garlic and cook for 1 min more, then tip in the celeriac and potato. Give everything a good stir and season with a big pinch of salt and white pepper. Pour in the stock, bring to the boil, then simmer for around 30 mins until the vegetables are completely soft.

STEP 3

Discard the herbs, then stir through the cream, remove from the heat and blitz until completely smooth. Stir through 1/2 tbsp truffle oil at a time and taste for seasoning – the strength of the oil will vary, so it's better to start with less oil and add a little at a time.

STEP 4

To serve, reheat the soup until piping hot, then ladle into bowls and top with the hazelnuts, some black pepper and an extra drizzle of truffle oil.

Gnocchi with herb sauce

Prep: 5 mins **Cook:** 5 mins

Serves 2-3

Ingredients

- 1 tbsp capers
- 4 anchovies (optional)
- 1 garlic clove
- 1 lemon, juiced and zested
- 50g herbs (we used parsley, chives and basil)
- 4 tbsp olive oil
- 500g gnocchi

Method

STEP 1

Blitz the capers, anchovies, garlic, lemon juice and herbs with 3 tbsp of the olive oil to make a sauce. Season and set aside.

STEP 2

Cook the gnocchi in salted water according to pack instructions, then drain. Heat the remaining oil in a non-stick frying pan over a high heat and add the gnocchi. Fry until crisp on the outside and warm all the way through – about 3 mins – remove from the pan and leave to drain on kitchen paper. Toss the gnocchi with the sauce, then divide between bowls, top with lemon zest and cracked black pepper to serve.

Curried parsnip soup shots

Prep: 10 mins **Cook:** 25 mins

Makes 12 shots

Ingredients

- 1 tbsp cold pressed rapeseed oil
- 1 onion , chopped
- ½ tbsp garam masala or curry powder
- 1 garlic clove , grated
- small piece ginger , grated
- 4 parsnips , peeled and sliced
- 600ml low-sodium veg stock

For the crispy kale topping

- 50g kale , torn into small pieces
- ½ tbsp cold pressed rapeseed oil
- ¼-½ tsp chilli powder

For the crispy prosciutto topping

- 1 slice prosciutto

Method

STEP 1

Heat oven to 180C/160C/gas 4. For the kale topping, massage the kale with the oil, chilli powder and a pinch of salt and pepper, then spread out on a baking tray. Roast for 8 mins until crisp, checking halfway through.

STEP 2

Heat the oil in a saucepan over a medium heat. Add the onion and fry until soft and lightly coloured, then add the garam masala (or curry powder), garlic and ginger. Cook for 1 min, then tip in the parsnips and stock. Bring to the boil, then simmer for 15 mins until the parsnip is completely soft. Blitz, adding enough water to get to your desired thickness, and season to taste.

STEP 3

To make the crispy prosciutto topping, put the prosciutto slice in a dry non-stick frying pan over a medium-high heat. Use a fish slice to keep it flat and fry for a couple of mins until crisp. Set aside to cool, then break into six pieces.

STEP 4

Divide the soup between 12 shot glasses. Top half with the roasted kale and the other half with the prosciutto.

Roasted stuffed cauliflower

Prep: 25 mins **Cook:** 1 hr and 5 mins

Serves 6

Ingredients

- 1 large or 2 small cauliflowers (about 850g)
- 5 tbsp olive oil
- 4 tbsp breadcrumbs

For the stuffing

- 250g kale , chopped
- 1 tbsp milled linseed
- 1 onion , chopped
- 2 garlic cloves , chopped
- ½ small pack sage , leaves chopped

- ½ small pack rosemary , leaves chopped
- 150g cooked chestnuts , finely chopped, plus 30g for the topping
- 2 lemons , zested
- good grating nutmeg

Method

STEP 1

Trim and discard the cauliflower leaves. Turn the cauliflower upside-down on a chopping board and use your knife to carefully cut out the stalk and core, leaving a cavity – the florets should still be holding together.

STEP 2

Bring a large pan of salted water to the boil. Submerge the cauliflower and cook for 7 mins, then remove with two slotted spoons and set aside to steam dry. Add the kale to the pan and cook for a min or so until wilted. Drain, then run under cold water to cool. Squeeze out the excess liquid and roughly chop.

STEP 3

To make a linseed 'egg' (this will bind the stuffing together), mix the ground linseed with 3 tbsp water and set aside for 5-10 mins until gluey. Meanwhile, heat 2 tbsp oil in a frying pan, add the onion and a pinch of salt, and cook until softened, then stir in the remaining stuffing ingredients, including the kale, and cook for a min or so more. Remove from the heat and season, then put in a blender with 150ml water and the linseed egg and blitz to a thick purée. Transfer to a piping bag.

STEP 4

Pipe the stuffing mixture into every nook and cranny of the cauliflower, getting in as much of the purée as you can – see our tip below. Transfer to a baking tray lined with parchment. Can be made up to this point in the morning and kept in the fridge.

STEP 5

Heat oven to 200C/180C fan/gas 6. Mix the remaining chestnuts with the breadcrumbs and some seasoning. Spoon the remaining oil all over the cauliflower, then pat on the breadcrumb chestnut mix. Roast for 45 mins until golden brown and tender (place under a hot grill for the last part of cooking time if it needs to crisp-up). Serve with any crisp bits that have fallen onto the baking tray.

Cauliflower, squash, coconut & lentil curry

Prep: 20 mins **Cook:** 1 hr and 10 mins

Serves 4

Ingredients

- 1 tbsp oil
- 1 onion , chopped
- 1 tbsp garam masala
- 1 tbsp turmeric
- 200g red lentils
- 400ml can coconut milk
- small bunch coriander , chopped
- cooked wholegrain basmati rice , to serve
- coconut yogurt (dairy free) , to serve

For the roast cauliflower & squash base

- 1 cauliflower , split into florets, the stalk cut into cubes
- ½ large butternut squash , cut into cubes
- 1 tbsp oil

Method

STEP 1

For the base, heat oven to 180C/160C fan/gas 4. Toss the cauliflower and squash in oil and spread it out on a large oven tray. Roast for 25 mins, or until tender. If you're making the base ahead of time, you can now freeze in an airtight container for up to a month. (Defrost fully before using in the next step.)

STEP 2

Heat oil in a pan, then add the onion and cook until soft, stir in the spices and cook for 2 mins. Stir in the lentils, coconut milk and 200ml water and bring to a simmer.

STEP 3

Cook for 20 mins, then add the roast veg and cook for a further 10 mins, adding a little water if it looks dry. Stir in the coriander. Serve with rice and yogurt.

Barbecue sesame sweet potatoes

Prep: 10 mins **Cook:** 1 hr

Serves 6

Ingredients

- 6 sweet potatoes , washed and cut into wedges
- 3 tbsp vegetable oil
- 1 tsp toasted sesame oil
- 1 tbsp ginger , chopped
- 1 garlic clove , chopped
- 3 tbsp soy sauce
- 1 lime , juiced
- 1 tbsp sesame seeds (black if you have them)
- 50g plain peanuts , crushed
- 1 green chilli , sliced
- ½ bunch of spring onions , washed and chopped

Method

STEP 1

Light a lidded barbecue. Let the flames die down and the coals turn ashen, then mound the coal up on one side or heat an oven to 180C/160C fan/gas 4. Arrange the sweet potatoes on a large tray and drizzle with 1 tbsp of the vegetable oil, season and toss. Cook on the barbecue or in the oven for 25 mins until charred and softened.

STEP 2

Meanwhile, whisk the remaining oils, ginger, garlic, soy and lime juice. Baste the potatoes with some of the sauce and return to the barbecue for another 30-40 mins, basting as they cook. Once the potatoes are glazed and sticky, remove and sprinkle on the sesame seeds and peanuts, and leave to cool slightly. Remove the wedges from the tray and pop into a salad bowl. Sprinkle over the chilli and spring onions and serve.

Quick hummus

Prep: 10 mins **Cook:** 2 mins

Serves 6

Ingredients

- 400g can chickpeas
- 100ml lemon juice
- 150ml olive oil
- 125g tahini
- 1 ½ tsp ground coriander
- 5 cardamom pods
- toasted pine nuts
- sumac

Method

STEP 1

Drain the can of chickpeas, keeping the water. Gently warm in a microwave, then tip into a food processor with the lemon juice, olive oil, tahini, ground coriander and crushed seeds from the cardamom pods. Blend until smooth – add a splash of chickpea water if it's looking a little dry. Check the seasoning and add more oil and lemon juice to taste. Serve sprinkled with toasted pine nuts and sumac.

Kidney bean curry

Prep: 5 mins **Cook:** 30 mins

Serves 2

Ingredients

- 1 tbsp vegetable oil
- 1 onion, finely chopped

- 2 garlic cloves, finely chopped
- thumb-sized piece of ginger, peeled and finely chopped
- 1 small pack coriander, stalks finely chopped, leaves roughly shredded
- 1 tsp ground cumin
- 1 tsp ground paprika
- 2 tsp garam masala
- 400g can chopped tomatoes
- 400g can kidney beans, in water
- cooked basmati rice, to serve

Method

STEP 1

Heat the oil in a large frying pan over a low-medium heat. Add the onion and a pinch of salt and cook slowly, stirring occasionally, until softened and just starting to colour. Add the garlic, ginger and coriander stalks and cook for a further 2 mins, until fragrant.

STEP 2

Add the spices to the pan and cook for another 1 min, by which point everything should smell aromatic. Tip in the chopped tomatoes and kidney beans in their water, then bring to the boil.

STEP 3

Turn down the heat and simmer for 15 mins until the curry is nice and thick. Season to taste, then serve with the basmati rice and the coriander leaves.

Thai red curry with quick pickled cucumber

Prep:25 mins **Cook:**35 mins

Serves 4

Ingredients

- 2 tsp vegetable oil
- 1 shallot, finely chopped
- 4 tbsp vegan Thai red curry paste
- 400ml Alpro coconut drink, unsweetened

- 400ml vegan vegetable stock
- 300g butternut squash, cut into 2cm cubes
- 150g baby potatoes, halved
- 150g green beans, trimmed
- 60g baby spinach leaves
- 100g shelled edamame beans
- 1 tbsp low sodium soy sauce or tamari
- 2 limes, juiced
- coriander or Thai basil leaves, to serve (optional)
- cooked brown rice, to serve

For the pickled cucumber

- 1 large cucumber
- 4 tbsp rice vinegar
- pinch of chilli flakes
- 2 tsp vegetable oil
- 1 shallot, finely chopped
- 4 tbsp vegan Thai red curry paste
- 400ml Alpro coconut drink, unsweetened
- 400ml vegan vegetable stock
- 300g butternut squash, cut into 2cm cubes
- 150g baby potatoes, halved
- 150g green beans, trimmed
- 60g baby spinach leaves
- 100g shelled edamame beans
- 1 tbsp low sodium soy sauce or tamari
- 2 limes, juiced
- coriander or Thai basil leaves, to serve (optional)
- cooked brown rice, to serve

For the pickled cucumber

- 1 large cucumber
- 4 tbsp rice vinegar
- pinch of chilli flakes

Method

STEP 1

To make the pickled cucumber, split the cucumber in half, remove the core with a teaspoon and discard. Cut the cucumber halves into thin semi-circles, then toss in a bowl with the vinegar, chilli and a pinch of salt. Leave to pickle while you make the curry.

STEP 2

Heat the oil in a deep frying pan over a medium heat. Add the shallot and fry for 5 mins until soft, then stir in the curry paste and cook for 2-3 mins until fragrant. Tip in the coconut milk and stock and bring to a simmer.

STEP 3

Add the squash and potatoes and cook uncovered for 20 mins until the potatoes are tender and the sauce has reduced and thickened slightly.

STEP 4

Stir in the green beans, spinach and edamame and cook for 4 mins more until tender. Season with the soy and lime juice and sprinkle over the coriander or Thai basil, if using. Serve in bowls over the rice with the pickled cucumber alongside.

STEP 5

To make the pickled cucumber, split the cucumber in half, remove the core with a teaspoon and discard. Cut the cucumber halves into thin semi-circles, then toss in a bowl with the vinegar, chilli and a pinch of salt. Leave to pickle while you make the curry.

STEP 6

Heat the oil in a deep frying pan over a medium heat. Add the shallot and fry for 5 mins until soft, then stir in the curry paste and cook for 2-3 mins until fragrant. Tip in the coconut milk and stock and bring to a simmer.

STEP 7

Add the squash and potatoes and cook uncovered for 20 mins until the potatoes are tender and the sauce has reduced and thickened slightly.

STEP 8

Stir in the green beans, spinach and edamame and cook for 4 mins more until tender. Season with the soy and lime juice and sprinkle over the coriander or Thai basil, if using. Serve in bowls over the rice with the pickled cucumber alongside.

Brussels sprouts pad Thai

Prep: 15 mins **Cook:** 10 mins

Serves 4

Ingredients

- 250g flat rice noodles (check the packet to make sure they're vegan)
- 1 tbsp soy sauce or tamari
- 1 tbsp tamarind paste (or 2 limes, juiced)
- 2 tsp palm sugar (or soft brown sugar)
- 2 tbsp vegetable oil
- 1 garlic clove , thinly sliced
- 2 spring onions , thinly sliced on a diagonal
- 1 red chilli , sliced
- 200g charred Brussels sprouts left over from Christmas Day, or cook from raw
- 100g beansprouts
- 30g salted peanuts (or any other nuts you might have), roughly chopped, to serve

lime wedges, to serve

Method

STEP 1

First, put the noodles in a large heatproof bowl, cover in boiling water and leave for 10 mins. Drain and rinse with cold water, then set aside. In a bowl, mix the soy sauce or tamari, tamarind or lime juice and sugar.

STEP 2

Heat the oil in a large frying pan or wok. Fry the garlic, spring onions, chilli and the cooked or leftover sprouts for around 2 mins (to cook the sprouts from raw, boil for 8-10 mins until tender). Then, add the noodles and beansprouts and fry for 1 min more. Pour over the sauce and toss well, working quickly to coat all the vegetables and noodles. Once everything is heated through, season and divide between four bowls. Scatter with the nuts and serve with lime wedges to squeeze over.

Cocoa & cherry oat bake

Prep: 15 mins **Cook:** 25 mins - 30 mins

Serves 6

Ingredients

- 75g dried cherries
- 1 tbsp chia seeds
- 500ml hazelnut milk
- 200g jumbo porridge oats
- 3 tbsp cocoa powder
- 1 tbsp cocoa nibs
- 1 tsp baking powder
- 1 tsp vanilla extract
- 50g blanched hazelnuts

fat-free yogurt and sugar-free cherry compote, to serve (optional)

Method

STEP 1

Heat the oven to 200C/180C fan/gas 6. Cover the cherries with boiling water and set aside for 10 mins. Meanwhile, mix the chia seeds with 3 tbsp warm water.

STEP 2

Drain the cherries and put in a large bowl with the soaked chia and the remaining ingredients, except the hazelnuts. Tip into a 2-litre ovenproof dish and scatter over the hazelnuts, then bake for 25-30 mins until piping hot in the middle. Serve with yogurt and cherry compote, if you like.

Raspberry ripple chia pudding

Prep: 15 mins

Serves 2

Ingredients

- 50g white chia seeds
- 200ml coconut drinking milk
- 1 nectarine or peach, cut into slices
- 2 tbsp goji berries

For the raspberry purée

- 100g raspberries
- 1 tsp lemon juice
- 2 tsp maple syrup

Method

STEP 1

Divide the chia seeds and coconut milk between two serving bowls and stir well. Leave to soak for 5 mins, stirring occasionally, until the seeds swell and thicken when stirred.

STEP 2

Meanwhile, combine the purée ingredients in a small food processor, or blitz with a hand blender. Swirl a spoonful into each bowl, then arrange the nectarine or peach slices on top and scatter with the goji berries. Will keep in the fridge for 1 day. Add the toppings just before serving.

Crispy sweet potatoes with chickpeas & tahini yogurt

Prep: 20 mins **Cook:** 1 hr

serves 4 as a side

Ingredients

- 4 medium sweet potatoes
- 4 tbsp olive oil
- 1 large garlic clove, crushed
- 1 banana shallot, finely chopped
- 400g can chickpeas, drained
- 75g baby leaf spinach

- small bunch dill , finely chopped
- zest and juice 1 lemon

For the tahini yogurt

- 60g Greek yogurt
- 2 tbsp tahini
- 20g pine nuts , toasted
- 110g pomegranate seeds

Method

STEP 1

Wrap each potato in foil and put directly on the hot coals of a barbecue for 35-45 mins, depending on the size of the potatoes. Insert a skewer into each one to check that they're cooked. (Alternatively, heat oven to 200C/180C fan/gas 6 and put the foil-wrapped potatoes on a large baking sheet. Bake in the oven for 45 mins-1 hr or until the centre is soft. Once cooked, put under a hot grill for 3 mins until the skin is blackened and crispy.)

STEP 2

Meanwhile, heat 1 tbsp olive oil in a large frying pan over a medium heat. Add the garlic and shallot and fry for 2-3 mins or until softened, then stir the chickpeas into the mixture. Gently warm through for 1 min or so, then add the spinach and leave to wilt. Add the dill.

STEP 3

Whisk together the lemon juice, zest and remaining olive oil in a small bowl. Season to taste and stir into the chickpea mixture. Gently mash with a potato masher until the chickpeas are slightly crushed. Mix together the yogurt and tahini in another small bowl, and season to taste with salt.

STEP 4

Split the potatoes open lengthways. Fill with the bean mixture, drizzle over the tahini yogurt and top with the pine nuts and pomegranate seeds.

Peach iced tea

Prep: 10 mins **Cook:** 5 mins

plus 1 hr infusing and chilling

Serves 12

Ingredients

- 200g granulated sugar
- 5 ripe peaches , 4 stoned and chopped, 1 sliced to serve
- 4 teabags

Method

STEP 1

Tip the sugar into a pan with 250ml water. Bring to the boil slowly, ensuring the sugar is fully dissolved. Add the chopped peaches and cook until very soft. Remove from the heat, mash the peaches with a fork, and leave to infuse for 1 hr.

STEP 2

Sieve the syrup through a fine sieve into a jug, mashing the fruit to release all the liquid. The syrup will keep in the fridge for one week.

STEP 3

Put the teabags in a large heatproof jug and pour over 2 litres boiling water. Leave to steep for 4 mins, then carefully remove the teabags. Leave to cool, then transfer to the fridge until chilled.

STEP 4

Stir the peach syrup into the iced tea with some ice, or pour a little of the syrup into tall glasses and add the tea. Top up with more water, sparkling water or ice. Add peach slices to serve.

Avocado on toast

Prep: 5 mins

Serves 1

Ingredients

- 1 ripe avocado
- ½ lemon

- big pinch chilli flakes
- 2 slices sourdough bread
- good drizzle extra virgin olive oil

Method

STEP 1

Cut the avocado in half and carefully remove its stone, then scoop out the flesh into a bowl. Squeeze in the lemon juice then mash with a fork to your desired texture. Season to taste with sea salt, black pepper and chilli flakes. Toast your bread, drizzle over the oil then pile the avocado on top.

Red pepper & bean tikka masala

Prep:10 mins **Cook:**20 mins

Serves 2

Ingredients

- 1 tbsp vegetable oil
- 1 onion , chopped
- 2 red peppers , deseeded and cut into strips
- 1 garlic clove , crushed
- thumb-sized piece of ginger , grated
- 1 red chilli , finely chopped
- ½ tbsp garam masala
- ½ tbsp curry powder
- 1 tbsp tomato purée
- 415g can baked beans
- ½ lemon , juiced

rice and coriander, to serve

Method

STEP 1

Heat the oil in a saucepan over a medium heat, add the onion and red peppers with a pinch of salt and fry until softened, around 5 mins. Tip in the garlic, ginger and red chilli along with the spices and fry for a couple of mins longer.

STEP 2

Spoon in the tomato purée, stir, then tip in the baked beans along with 100ml water. Bubble for 5 mins, then squeeze in the lemon juice. Serve with the rice and scatter over the coriander leaves.

Pear, pumpkin & ginger juice mocktail

Prep: 10 mins

Serves 2

Ingredients

- tube of black icing
- 50g pumpkin or butternut squash, peeled and deseeded
- 1 ripe pear
- 250ml orange juice
- 1cm thick slice ginger

Method

STEP 1

Decorate two tumblers to look like Halloween pumpkins with the tube of black icing – pipe triangles for the eyes and noses and zig zags for the mouths. Leave to dry. Cut the pumpkin into smaller chunks and put in a blender along with the pear, orange juice, ginger and 100ml cold water. Blend until smooth then pour into the prepared glasses.

Slow cooker ratatouille

Prep: 10 mins **Cook:** 6 hrs and 20 mins

Serves 6

Ingredients

- 2 tbsp olive oil
- 1 red onion, sliced
- 2 garlic cloves
- 2 large aubergines, cut into 1.5cm pieces
- 3 courgettes, halved and cut into 2cm pieces
- 3 mixed peppers, cut into 2cm pieces
- 1 tbsp tomato purée
- 6 large ripe tomatoes, roughly chopped
- small bunch of basil, roughly chopped, plus a few extra leaves to serve
- few thyme sprigs
- 400g can plum tomatoes
- 1 tbsp red wine vinegar
- 1 tsp brown sugar
- sourdough, to serve (optional)

Method

STEP 1

Heat the oil in a large frying pan and fry the onion for 8 mins until translucent. Add the garlic and fry for 1 min. Turn the heat to medium-high, add the aubergines and fry for 5 mins until golden. Stir in the courgettes and peppers and fry for 5 mins more until slightly soft. Add the tomato purée, fresh tomatoes, herbs, canned tomatoes, vinegar, sugar and 1 tsp salt and bring to the boil.

STEP 2

Transfer to the slow cooker and cook on low for 5-6 hours or until everything is soft and the sauce has thickened. Season, scatter over some extra basil, and serve with sourdough, if you like.

Leek, pea & watercress soup

Prep: 10 mins **Cook:** 22 mins

Serves 4

Ingredients

- 1 tbsp olive oil , plus a drizzle to serve
- 2 leeks , finely sliced
- 4 small garlic cloves , crushed
- 650-800ml hot veg stock
- 80g watercress
- 400g frozen peas
- 1 small lemon , zested and juiced
- small bunch of parsley , finely chopped

dairy-free crème fraîche and crusty bread, to serve (optional)

Method

STEP 1

Heat the oil in a large saucepan over a medium heat. Add the leeks and garlic and fry for 7-10 mins or until softened and translucent.

STEP 2

Pour in the hot stock and simmer for 5-10 mins. Stir through the watercress, reserving a few leaves for garnish, then the peas, and cook for 5 mins until wilted. Use a hand blender or processor and whizz until smooth. Stir through the lemon juice and zest, then season to taste. Stir through half the parsley. Ladle into bowls and top with the remaining parsley, reserved watercress and a drizzle of olive oil. Swirl through some crème fraîche, then serve with crusty bread, if you like.

Crunchy parsnips

Prep: 15 mins **Cook:** 40 mins

Serves 8

Ingredients

- 2kg parsnips , peeled, trimmed and cut into halves or quarters lengthways
- 100ml rapeseed or sunflower oil
- 5 tbsp polenta
- 2 tsp paprika

Method

STEP 1

Heat the oven to 220C/200C fan/gas 7. Blanch the parsnips in boiling water for 4-5 mins until slightly soft. Drain, leave to steam-dry, then tip into a large bowl. Drizzle over the oil and toss to coat all the parsnips.

STEP 2

Mix the polenta, 2 tsp sea salt, 1 tsp ground black pepper and the paprika, and sprinkle over the parsnips. Toss well, then lay the parsnips out on one large baking tray (or two small ones), with lots of space between them. Roast for 15 mins, turn them over, then roast for another 20-25 mins until golden and crunchy.

Avocado & cannellini bean dip

Prep: 10 mins

Serves 4

Ingredients

- 1 small avocado
- 400g can cannellini beans , drained
- 1 garlic clove , finely grated
- ½ tsp chilli flakes , plus extra to serve
- ½ tsp ground cumin
- 1 lemon , zested and juiced
- 3 tbsp avocado oil , plus extra for drizzling

mixed seeds , crackers or crudités, to serve (optional)

Method

STEP 1

Scoop the avocado flesh into a blender or small food processor. Add the beans, garlic, spices, lemon zest and juice and oil. Blitz until completely smooth, loosening with 50-100ml water, if needed. Season.

STEP 2

Spoon into a bowl and top with extra chilli flakes and avocado oil. Serve with the seeds scattered over, and crackers or crudités, if you like.

Sweet potato, peanut butter & chilli quesadillas

Prep: 15 mins **Cook:** 45 mins

Serves 2

Ingredients

- 3 medium sweet potatoes peeled and thinly sliced
- 1 tbsp smoked paprika
- 3 tbsp olive oil , plus extra for brushing
- 1 extra large ripe avocado
- ½ lime , zested and juiced, plus wedges to serve
- 2 tbsp crunchy peanut butter
- 4 small flour tortillas
- sriracha chilli sauce , to taste
- ½ small pack coriander , torn

Method

STEP 1

Heat oven to 200C/180C fan/gas 6. Toss the sweet potatoes with the paprika and 2 tbsp olive oil in a roasting tin. Roast for 15 mins, tossing halfway through, until the potatoes are beginning to crisp.

STEP 2

Stone, peel and chop the avocado, tip into a bowl with the lime juice and zest, and season generously. Mash together with a fork and set aside. In a small bowl, combine the peanut butter and remaining olive oil. Set aside.

STEP 3

Heat a griddle pan or frying pan over a medium heat until very hot. Brush each tortilla on one side with the remaining oil. Place one tortilla, oiled-side down, in the pan and spread over half the peanut butter mixture, half the sweet potatoes, a little chilli sauce and half the coriander. Top with another tortilla, oiled-side up. Press down with a heavy saucepan and cook for 2-3 mins each side until the quesadilla is crisp outside and warm in the middle. Repeat to make a second quesadilla, then cut each into quarters and serve with the crushed avocado and lime wedges.

Pumpkin seed butter

Prep: 10 mins

Makes 500ml jar

Ingredients

- 500g pumpkin seeds
- 1 tbsp maple syrup (optional)

Method

STEP 1

Put the seeds in a food processor and blitz for 5-8 mins, scraping the sides down as you go. Try not to let it overheat – if the mixture feels too warm, leave it for a little longer between intervals. It should be thick and spreadable.

STEP 2

To sweeten, mix in the maple syrup, if you like. Put in a sterile jar and chill for up to one week.

Spinach & chickpea dhal

Prep: 10 mins **Cook:** 25 mins

Serves 2

Ingredients

- 400g can chickpeas
- 200g bag spinach
- 160ml can coconut cream
- 1 tbsp aubergine pickle

Method

STEP 1

Heat oven to 220C/200C fan/gas 7. Drain the chickpeas, reserving the liquid, then tip ½ of them onto a baking tray, season, drizzle over 2 tsp sunflower oil and roast for 15 mins. Wilt the spinach in a frying pan with 1 tsp sunflower oil, then add the coconut cream, remaining chickpeas and pickle. Mix well and simmer for 3-4 mins, squashing the chickpeas with the back of a spoon. Add a splash of the chickpea liquid if it looks dry. Sprinkle the roasted chickpeas on top and serve with naan bread.

Parsnip gnocchi

Prep: 40 mins **Cook:** 55 mins

Serves 4

Ingredients

- 400g parsnip , peeled and cut into chunks
- 600g potatoes , peeled and cut into chunks
- 60ml olive oil , plus a drizzle to serve
- 3 unpeeled garlic cloves
- 1 tsp ground nutmeg (around 1 clove)
- 100g '00' flour
- 2 tbsp nutritional yeast
- ½ small pack thyme , leaves picked, to serve
- 30g walnuts , toasted and chopped, to serve

Method

STEP 1

Heat oven to 220C/200C fan/gas 7. Toss the parsnips and potatoes in 2 tbsp of the olive oil and tip into a roasting tin along with the garlic cloves. Roast for 40 mins or until the veg is completely soft. Remove from the oven and leave to cool a little. Squeeze the garlic from their skins, then discard the skins. Tip everything into a food processor, along with the nutmeg, flour and nutritional yeast, season well, then pulse until well combined and holding together as a dough.

STEP 2

Bring a large pan of salted water to the boil. Tip the dough onto a floured surface, cut into four chunks and roll each into a sausage about 35cm long and 2.5cm wide. Use the back of a table knife to cut each sausage into small pillow-shaped gnocchi, each around 2cm long. Cook the gnocchi in batches for 1 min or until they float to the surface. Remove from the water with a slotted spoon and drain on kitchen paper.

STEP 3

In a frying pan, heat the rest of the oil over a medium heat until shimmering. Add half the gnocchi and fry until lightly golden on each side, around 3-4 mins. Transfer them to a tray using a slotted spoon while you cook the second batch. When all the gnocchi are golden, return them all to the pan to warm through before dividing between four plates. Sprinkle over some black pepper, then top with the thyme leaves, toasted walnuts and a drizzle of olive oil, if you like.

Chilli & avocado salsa sweet potatoes

Prep: 15 mins **Cook:** 45 mins

Serves 2

Ingredients

- 2 large sweet potatoes
- 1 tbsp vegetable oil
- 1 onion , finely chopped
- 2 garlic cloves , crushed
- 1 tsp paprika
- 400g can chopped tomatoes
- 1 small avocado , chopped
- 1 red chilli , finely chopped
- ½ small pack coriander , chopped
- 400g can mixed beans , drained
- ½ x 460g jar roasted red peppers , sliced

1 tbsp coconut yogurt , to serve (optional)

Method

STEP 1

Heat oven to 200C/180C fan/gas 6. Prick the sweet potatoes with a fork and bake for 40-45 mins, or until tender and cooked.

STEP 2

Meanwhile, heat the oil in a deep frying pan and cook the onion for about 10 mins until softening. Add the garlic and paprika, and stir for 1 min. Tip in the tomatoes, then bring to a gentle simmer, season well and leave to bubble away for 10-15 mins.

STEP 3

To make the salsa, combine the avocado, chilli and coriander in a small bowl. Pour the mixed beans into the pan with the red peppers. Warm through for 5 mins and taste.

STEP 4

Halve each baked potato, ladle over the chilli and spoon on the salsa. Add a dollop of coconut yogurt to each half before serving, if you like.

Fruity mocktail

Prep: 5 mins

Serves 4

Ingredients

- handful of green grapes
- handful of blueberries
- 4 tbsp grenadine
- 300-400ml orange juice
- sparkling water , to top up

You will need

- 4 bamboo skewers

Method

STEP 1

Thread the grapes and blueberries onto the skewers to make stirrers.

STEP 2

Pour the grenadine into four glasses. Gently tip the glasses and pour the orange juice down the inside of the glasses so it sits on top of the grenadine. Top up with sparking water, and add the stirrers to serve.

Cranberry & lentil bake

Prep: 5 mins **Cook:** 25 mins

Serves 1

Ingredients

- 25g dried cranberries
- 1 tbsp red wine
- 125g cooked puy lentils
- 2 tsp olive oil
- ½ onion, finely chopped
- ½ garlic clove, crushed or finely grated
- 1 tbsp chopped sage
- ½ tbsp chopped parsley
- ¼ tsp smoked paprika
- pinch ground cloves
- 1 tsp tomato purée
- 1 tsp soy sauce
- 1 tsp cornflour

Method

STEP 1

Heat oven to 200C/180C fan/gas 6. Oil and line the base of a 200ml ovenproof ramekin with a circle of baking parchment. Put the cranberries in a small pan with the wine and cook for a couple of mins over a medium heat until the cranberries are plump and the wine syrupy. Pour into the base of the ramekin and set aside.

STEP 2

Put the lentils in a bowl and roughly mash about half of them with a fork. Heat the oil in a small pan and cook the onion for 6-8 mins over a medium heat until softened. Stir in the garlic, herbs, paprika and cloves and cook for another minute. Turn off the heat and add the lentils, tomato purée, soy and cornflour, stir everything together well, then spoon into the ramekin, pressing down gently with the back of a spoon. Can be chilled for two days, or freeze for up to two months, with the ramekin covered. Defrost in the fridge before cooking.

STEP 3

Put the ramekin on a baking tray and bake for 15 mins. Leave to cool for 1 min, then turn out onto a plate.

Nut roast

Prep: 30 mins **Cook:** 1 hr and 5 mins

Serves 4

Ingredients

- 1 tbsp olive oil
- 15g butter
- 1 large onion, finely chopped
- 2 sticks celery, finely chopped
- 2 garlic cloves, finely chopped
- 200g chestnut mushrooms, finely chopped
- 1 red pepper, halved, deseeded and finely diced
- 1 large carrot, grated
- 1 tsp dried oregano
- 1 tsp smoked paprika
- 100g red lentils
- 2 tbsp tomato purée
- 300ml vegetable stock
- 100g fresh breadcrumbs
- 150g mixed nuts such as walnuts, pecans, hazelnuts and Brazil nuts, roughly chopped
- 3 large eggs, lightly beaten
- 100g mature cheddar, grated
- handful flat-leaf parsley, finely chopped

For the tomato sauce

- 2 tbsp extra virgin olive oil

- 2 garlic cloves, finely sliced
- 1 sprig rosemary
- 400ml passata

Method

STEP 1

Heat the oven to 180C/ fan 160C/ gas 4 and line the base and sides of a 1.5 litre loaf tin with parchment paper.

STEP 2

Heat 1 tbsp olive oil and 15g butter in a large frying pan and cook 1 finely chopped large onion and 2 finely chopped celery sticks for about 5 mins until beginning to soften.

STEP 3

Stir in 2 finely chopped garlic cloves and 200g finely chopped chestnut mushrooms and cook for a further 10 mins.

STEP 4

Stir in 1 finely diced red pepper and 1 grated carrot and cook for about 3 mins then add 1 tsp dried oregano and 1 tsp smoked paprika and cook for just a minute.

STEP 5

Add 100g red lentils and 2 tbsp tomato purée and cook for about 1 min, then add 300ml vegetable stock and simmer over a very gentle heat until all the liquid has been absorbed and the mixture is fairly dry. This should take about 25 minutes. Set aside to cool.

STEP 6

Finally, stir in 100g fresh breadcrumbs, 150g chopped mixed nuts, 3 lightly beaten large eggs, 100g grated mature cheddar, a handful of finely chopped flat-leaf parsley and a pinch of salt and some ground black pepper.

STEP 7

Stir to mix well then spoon the mixture into the prepared tin and press down the surface.

STEP 8

Cover with foil and bake for 30 mins, then remove the foil and bake for a further 20 mins until firm when pressed gently.

STEP 9

Meanwhile, to make the sauce, heat 2 tbsp extra virgin olive oil very gently then add 2 finely sliced garlic cloves and 1 rosemary sprig and heat without colouring.

STEP 10

Pour in 400ml passata and add a pinch of salt and some ground black pepper. Simmer gently for just 15 mins.

STEP 11

Allow the loaf to cool in the tin for about 10 mins then turn out onto a serving board or plate. Remove the baking paper and cut into slices and serve with a little of the tomato sauce.

STEP 12

To make a vegan nut roast, use an extra tbsp of oil in place of butter, no cheese and 3 tbsp egg replacer. Bake your nut roast for 1 hour. The loaf will still be soft in the middle after cooking.

STEP 13

It can be cooked in advance and then chilled, sliced and reheated to make it easier to serve.

Chilli tempeh stir-fry

Prep: 10 mins **Cook:** 15 mins

Serves 2

Ingredients

- 300g long-stem broccoli
- ½ tbsp toasted sesame oil
- 150g tempeh, sliced and cut into 2cm cubes
- 2 garlic cloves, thinly sliced
- 1 thumb-sized piece ginger, peeled and finely grated
- ½ small red chilli, deseeded and finely chopped
- ½ tbsp gochujang paste

- 1 tsp sesame seeds

steamed brown rice , to serve (optional)

Method

STEP 1

Boil the broccoli for 1 min 30 secs. Drain.

STEP 2

Heat the oil in a non-stick pan. Stir-fry the tempeh for 2-3 mins, then put on a plate. Fry the garlic, ginger and chilli for 2 mins. Tip in the broccoli and toss.

STEP 3

Mix the gochujang with 2 tbsp water and the tempeh. Add to the pan with the seeds. Cook for 2 mins. Serve with rice, if you like.

Autumn vegetable salad with saffron dressing

Prep: 35 mins **Cook:** 15 mins

Serves 6 as a side

Ingredients

- 12 rainbow carrots , tops left on, washed and peeled
- 1 medium courgette , sliced
- 8 stalks long-stem broccoli , any thick stalks halved lengthways
- 1 tbsp rapeseed oil
- 100g mixed cherry tomatoes , halved
- 4 spring onions , thinly sliced at an angle
- 3 plum tomatoes , scored, blanched, peeled, deseeded and cut into small pieces
- handful black olives , stoned and sliced
- ½ cucumber , cut lengthways, seeds removed and sliced at the angle
- 3 tbsp roughly chopped basil

For the dressing

- 20ml cider vinegar

- ½ tsp Dijon mustard
- pinch saffron strands
- 1 tsp caster sugar
- 50ml extra virgin rapeseed oil
- 1 small shallot , finely chopped

Method

STEP 1

Heat a griddle pan over a medium-high heat. Tip the carrots, courgettes and broccoli into a large mixing bowl, lightly season and toss together with the rapeseed oil. Once the griddle is hot, add the vegetables in batches and leave to slightly char for around 3-4 mins, then transfer back to the bowl. When all the veg is charred, add the remaining salad ingredients, toss together and set aside.

STEP 2

To make the saffron dressing, whisk the vinegar, mustard, saffron and sugar together in a bowl with a pinch of salt until the sugar has dissolved. Whisk in the oil gradually, then stir in the shallots. Dress the salad and serve.

Squash steaks with chestnut & cavolo nero pilaf

Prep: 10 mins **Cook:** 55 mins

Serves 4

Ingredients

- 1 butternut squash
- 2-3 tbsp olive oil , plus extra for frying
- ½ tsp smoked paprika , plus a little extra for sprinkling
- 200g cavolo nero or curly kale, shredded
- 1 onion , chopped
- 180g chestnuts , halved
- 2 garlic cloves , finely chopped
- ½ tsp ground cumin
- ½ tsp ground cinnamon
- 250g basmati rice & wild rice

- 500ml vegetable stock
- 150g pot of coconut yogurt

Method

STEP 1

Heat oven to 220C/200C fan/ gas 7. Cut the neck of the squash into four rounds (keep the rest for another time). Heat the oil in a frying pan and brown the squash for a few mins each side. Transfer to a baking tray, sprinkle with half the paprika and roast for 30 mins.

STEP 2

Meanwhile, in the same frying pan, add a little extra oil and stir-fry the cavolo nero for 2 mins, then remove with a slotted spoon and set aside. Add the onion and chestnuts to the pan, cook for a few mins, then stir in the garlic, remaining paprika and spices and cook for 1 min. Stir in the rice and stock, bring to the boil, then cover with a lid. Turn the heat down as low as it will go and cook for 25 mins, stirring occasionally.

STEP 3

Once cooked, stir through the cavolo nero and serve with the squash steaks and the coconut yogurt sprinkled with paprika.

Roast asparagus bowls with tahini lemon dressing

Prep: 15 mins **Cook:** 25 mins

Serves 2

Ingredients

- 2 red onions , halved and thickly sliced
- 2 tsp rapeseed oil
- 250g pack asparagus , woody ends trimmed
- 160g cherry tomatoes
- 2 tbsp sunflower seeds
- 1 tsp vegetable bouillon powder
- 120g quinoa
- 2 tsp tahini
- ½ lemon , juiced

- 1 large garlic clove , finely grated
- 2 tsp tamari
- 2 good handfuls rocket
- 400g aduki beans in water, drained

Method

STEP 1

Heat oven to 220C/200C fan/gas 7. Toss the onions in 1 tsp rapeseed oil and roast on a baking sheet for 10 mins. Coat the asparagus with the remaining oil and spread over another sheet. After 10 mins, add the asparagus to roast with the onions for 5 mins. Add the tomatoes and sunflower seeds and roast for 5 mins. The onions should be charred, the asparagus tender, the seeds toasted and the whole tomatoes near bursting.

STEP 2

Meanwhile, tip the bouillon and quinoa into a pan. Add 360ml water, cover and simmer for 20 mins until tender and the water has been absorbed. Whisk the tahini and lemon juice with 3 tbsp warm water, the garlic and tamari to make a dressing.

STEP 3

Pile the quinoa into bowls, top with rocket, spoon over half the dressing, add a pile of beans with the tomatoes, then a separate pile of the asparagus and onions. Spoon over the remaining dressing and scatter over the sunflower seeds. Will keep in the fridge for two days.

Sweet potato & black bean chilli with zesty quinoa

Prep: 25 mins **Cook:** 45 mins

Serves 3

Ingredients

- 1 tbsp rapeseed oil
- 2 sweet potatoes , peeled and cut into 1 in cubes
- 1 onion , chopped
- 2 fat garlic cloves crushed
- 1 red chilli , seeds removed if you don't like it too hot, and finely chopped
- small bunch coriander , stalks finely chopped, leaves roughly chopped (keep them separate)

- 2 tsp ground coriander
- 2 tsp ground cumin
- 2 tsp smoked paprika
- 2 tsp chipotle paste (ensure you use a gluten-free variety)
- 1 heaped tsp vegan-friendly yeast extract
- 2 x 400g cans chopped tomato
- 400g can black bean
- 140g quinoa , cooked according to pack instructions, or 250g pack ready-cooked quinoa (we used Merchant Gourmet red and white quinoa)
- zest and juice 1 lime
- 1 tbsp pumpkin seed
- 1 ripe avocado , peeled and cubed

Method

STEP 1

Heat oven to 180C/160C fan/gas 4. Toss the potatoes with half the oil and some seasoning on a baking tray. Bake for 30 mins, tossing halfway through cooking, until tender. Meanwhile, heat the remaining oil in a pan, add the onion and cook for 5 mins until soft, then add the garlic, chilli and coriander stalks. Cook everything for a further 2-3 mins, stirring to prevent the garlic from burning. Sprinkle in the spices, stirring for 1 min more, until aromatic. Stir in the chipotle paste, yeast extract, tomatoes and half a can of water, swirling it around the tin to wash out all the bits of tomato. Simmer the sauce, uncovered, while the sweet potato is cooking, adding a splash more water if it looks too dry.

STEP 2

Add the sweet potato, black beans and seasoning to the chilli. Bubble for 5 mins, then taste and adjust the seasoning with a squeeze of lime and a sprinkle of sugar if it needs it. Meanwhile, stir the lime zest, a squeeze of lime juice, the coriander leaves and the pumpkin seeds into the quinoa. Toss the avocado in the remaining lime juice as soon as you've cut it – this will prevent it turning brown. To serve, divide the quinoa between plates or bowls, top with the chilli and a pile of avocado.

Peanut butter overnight oats

Prep: 5 mins

Serves 1

Ingredients

- 80g frozen raspberries
- 50g rolled porridge oats
- 1 tsp maple syrup
- 1 tbsp peanut butter

Method

STEP 1

Stir the frozen raspberries into your oats with 150ml water and a pinch of salt, then cover and chill in the fridge overnight.

STEP 2

The next day, mix in the maple syrup, then top the oats with the peanut butter.

Barley & broccoli risotto with lemon & basil

Prep: 10 mins **Cook:** 35 mins

Serves 2

Ingredients

- 100g wholegrain pearl barley
- 2 tsp reduced-salt vegetable bouillon powder
- 2 tbsp rapeseed oil
- 1 large leek , chopped
- 2 garlic cloves
- ⅔ pack basil
- generous squeeze of lemon juice
- 125g Tenderstem broccoli from a 200g pack

Method

STEP 1

Pour a litre of cold water over the barley, cover and leave to soak overnight.

STEP 2

The next day, drain the barley, reserve the liquid and use it to make 500ml vegetable bouillon. Heat half the oil in a non-stick pan, add the leek and cook briefly to soften. Tip half into a bowl, then add the barley and bouillon to the pan, cover and simmer for 20 mins.

STEP 3

Meanwhile, add the garlic, basil, remaining oil, the lemon juice and 3 tbsp water to the leeks in the bowl, and blitz to a paste with a stick blender

STEP 4

When the barley has cooked for 20 mins, add the broccoli to the pan and cook for 5-10 mins more until both are tender. Stir in the basil purée, heat very briefly (to retain the fragrance), then spoon into bowls to serve.

Roasted root & chickpea salad

Prep: 25 mins **Cook:** 50 mins

Serves 4

Ingredients

- 4 carrots , peeled and cut into rough chunks
- 1 celeriac , peeled and cut into rough chunks
- 1 butternut squash , peeled and cut into rough chunks
- 1 tbsp smoked paprika
- 1 tbsp ground cumin
- 1 tsp cinnamon
- 1 tsp turmeric
- 4 tbsp cold pressed rapeseed oil
- 4 raw beetroot , peeled and cut into rough chunks
- 2 x 400g cans chickpeas , drained and rinsed
- 1 small red onion , thinly sliced
- 2 tbsp red wine vinegar (check the label if you're vegan)
- pinch of sugar

- 1 small pack coriander , roughly chopped
- 1 small pack mint , roughly chopped
- 50g almonds , toasted and roughly chopped

Method

STEP 1

Heat oven to 220C/200C fan/gas 7. Put the carrots, celeriac and squash in a large bowl. Sprinkle over ¾ of the spices and ¾ of the oil. Toss to combine and season. Transfer to two large roasting trays. Add the beetroot to the same bowl, and toss in the remaining oil, spices and some seasoning, then divide between the roasting trays (coating the beetroot separately will stop everything turning purple). Roast the veg for 45 mins or until tender, tossing halfway. Add the chickpeas to the tray, stir, then return to the oven for 5 mins.

STEP 2

Meanwhile, mix the onion with the vinegar, sugar and some seasoning. Set aside to pickle.

STEP 3

Transfer the roasted vegetables to a sharing platter, stir through the pickled onions and their vinegar, the herbs and almonds, and serve.

Chive waffles with maple & soy mushrooms

Prep: 25 mins **Cook:** 20 mins

Serves 6

Ingredients

- 500ml soya milk or rice milk
- 1 tsp cider vinegar or lemon juice
- 2 tbsp rapeseed oil
- 100g cooked, mashed sweet potato
- 150g polenta
- 130g plain flour
- 1 tbsp baking powder
- small bunch chives , snipped
- 1 tbsp maple syrup

- 2 tsp light soy sauce
- 6 large mushrooms , thickly sliced
- olive oil , for frying
- soya yogurt , to serve (optional)

Method

STEP 1

Heat the waffle iron. Mix the soya or rice milk with the vinegar and rapeseed oil (don't worry if it starts to split), then whisk in the sweet potato mash. Tip the polenta, flour and baking powder into a bowl, mix and make a well in the centre. Add a large pinch of salt, then slowly pour in the milk mixture and whisk to make a batter. Stir in half the chives.

STEP 2

Pour enough batter into the waffle iron to fill and cook for 4-5 mins. Lift out the waffle, keep it warm and repeat with the remaining mixture until you have six waffles.

STEP 3

Meanwhile, mix the maple syrup with the soy sauce. Brush it over the mushrooms and season with pepper. Heat a little oil in a frying pan and fry the mushrooms on both sides until they are browned and cooked through – make sure they don't burn at the edges. Serve the waffles topped with mushrooms, add a spoonful of soya yogurt, if you like, and scatter over the remaining chives.

Creamy squash linguine

Prep:5 mins Cook:1 hr

Serves 4

Ingredients

350g chopped butternut squash

3 peeled garlic cloves

3 tbsp olive oil

350g linguine

small bunch sage

Method

STEP 1

Heat oven to 200C/180C fan/gas 6. Put the squash and garlic on a baking tray and drizzle with the olive oil. Roast for 35-40 mins until soft. Season.

STEP 2

Cook the pasta according to pack instructions. Drain, reserving the water. Use a stick blender to whizz the squash with 400ml cooking water. Heat some oil in a frying pan, fry the sage until crisp, then drain on kitchen paper. Tip the pasta and sauce into the pan and warm through. Scatter with sage.

Sourdough starter

Makes 2 loaves (12-15 slices each)

Ingredients

250g strong white bread flour , preferably organic or stoneground

Method

STEP 1

Day 1:
To begin your starter, mix 50g flour with 50g tepid water in a jar or, better still, a plastic container. Make sure all the flour is incorporated and leave, semi-uncovered, at room temperature for 24 hrs.

STEP 2

Day 2:
Mix 50g flour with 50g tepid water and stir into yesterday's mixture. Make sure all the flour is incorporated and leave, semi-uncovered, at room temperature for another 24 hrs.

STEP 3

Day 3:

Mix 50g flour with 50g tepid water and stir into yesterday's mixture. Make sure all the flour is incorporated and leave, semi-uncovered, at room temperature for another 24 hrs.

STEP 4

Day 4:

You should start to see some activity in the mixture now; there should be some bubbles forming and bubbling on top. Mix 50g flour with 50g tepid water and stir into yesterday's mixture. Make sure all the flour is incorporated and leave, semi-uncovered, at room temperature for another 24 hrs.

STEP 5

Day 5:

The mixture should be very active now and ready for making your levain (starter). If it's not bubbling, continue to feed it on a daily basis until it does. When it's ready, it should smell like yogurt.

STEP 6

You now have a starter, which is the base to the bread. You'll need to look after it, but naming is optional! Keep it in the fridge (it will stay dormant) and 24 hrs before you want to use it, pour half of it off and feed it with 100g flour and 100g water. Leave it at room temperature and it should become active again. The longer the starter has been dormant, the more times it will need to be refreshed – the process of pouring off half the starter and replacing it with new flour and water – to reactivate. If your starter is ready to use, a teaspoonful of the mixture should float in warm water.
The starter can now be used to make white sourdough bread.

Carrot & caraway crackers

Prep: 20 mins **Cook:** 15 mins

Makes 20

Ingredients

- 2 tbsp olive oil
- 1 shallot , roughly chopped
- 1 garlic clove , roughly chopped

- 1 tsp caraway seeds
- 400g carrots, roughly chopped
- 300ml vegan vegetable stock
- 20 crunchy vegan crackers (such as an olive oil toast)
- ½ small pack dill, leaves picked, to serve
- 20 veg crisps (we used a small bag of Tyrells), to serve

Method

STEP 1

Heat the oil in a saucepan over a medium heat. Add the shallot and a pinch of salt, and cook for 6 mins until softened. Stir in the garlic and caraway seeds and cook for 1 min more, then add the carrot and veg stock, bring to a boil and simmer for 12 mins.

STEP 2

Once the carrots are completely soft, drain them (reserve the liquid) and blitz to a smooth purée – add a tbsp of the reserved stock initially, but use more if necessary to get the desired consistency. Season and leave to cool. The purée can be made a day ahead and kept in the fridge.

STEP 3

To serve, spoon the purée – or, if you want to be extra fancy, transfer it to a piping bag and pipe it – onto the oatcakes and top each with a little dill and a veg crisp.

Curried tofu wraps

Prep: 20 mins **Cook:** 25 mins

Serves 4

Ingredients

- ½ red cabbage (about 500g), shredded
- 4 heaped tbsp dairy-free yogurt (we used Alpro Plain with Coconut)
- 3 tbsp mint sauce
- 3 x 200g packs tofu, each cut into 15 cubes
- 2 tbsp tandoori curry paste
- 2 tbsp oil

- 2 onions, sliced
- 2 large garlic cloves, sliced
- 8 chapatis
- 2 limes, cut into quarters

Method

STEP 1

Mix the cabbage, yogurt and mint sauce, season and set aside. Toss the tofu with the tandoori paste and 1 tbsp of the oil. Heat a frying pan and cook the tofu, in batches, for a few mins each side until golden. Remove from the pan with a slotted spoon and set aside. Add the remaining oil to the pan, stir in the onions and garlic, and cook for 8-10 mins until softened. Return the tofu to the pan and season well.

STEP 2

Warm the chapatis following pack instructions, then top each one with some cabbage, followed by the curried tofu and a good squeeze of lime.

Aubergine & chickpea bites

Prep: 20 mins **Cook:** 1 hr

Makes 20

Ingredients

- 3 large aubergines, halved, cut side scored
- spray oil
- 2 fat garlic cloves, peeled
- 2 tsp coriander
- 2 tsp cumin seeds
- 400g can chickpeas, drained
- 2 tbsp gram flour
- 1 lemon, ½ zested and juice, ½ cut into wedges to serve (optional)
- 3 tbsp polenta

For the dip

- 1 tbsp harissa (we used Belazu rose harissa)
- 150g coconut dairy-free yogurt (we used Coyo)

Method

STEP 1

Heat oven to 200C/180C fan/gas 6. Spray the aubergine halves generously with oil, then put them cut-side up in a large roasting tin with the garlic, coriander and cumin seeds. Season, then roast for 40 mins until the aubergine is completely tender. Set aside to cool a little.

STEP 2

Scoop the aubergine flesh into a bowl and discard the skins. Use a spatula to scrape the spices and garlic into the bowl. Add the chickpeas, gram flour, lemon zest and juice, roughly mash together and check the seasoning. Don't worry if the mix is a bit soft – it will firm up in the fridge.

STEP 3

Shape the mixture into 20 balls and put them on a baking tray lined with baking parchment, then leave to chill in the fridge for at least 30 mins. Swirl the harissa through the yogurt and set aside. Can make ahead to this point the day before and kept covered in the fridge.

STEP 4

Heat oven to 180C/160C fan/gas 4. Tip the polenta onto a plate, roll the balls in it to coat, then return them to the tray and spray each one with a little oil. Roast for 20 mins until crisp, hot and golden. Serve with the harissa yogurt and lemon wedges, if you like.

Sticky tofu with noodles

Prep: 25 mins **Cook:** 25 mins

Serves 2

Ingredients

- ½ large cucumber
- 100ml rice wine vinegar
- 2 tbsp golden caster sugar
- 100ml vegetable oil

- 200g pack firm tofu , cut into 3cm cubes
- 2 tbsp maple syrup
- 4 tbsp brown or white miso paste
- 30g white sesame seeds
- 250g dried soba noodles (we used buckwheat)
- 2 spring onions , shredded, to serve

Method

STEP 1

Using a peeler, cut thin ribbons off the cucumber, leaving the seeds behind. Put the ribbons in a bowl and set aside. Gently heat the vinegar, sugar, 1/4 tsp salt and 100ml water in a saucepan over a medium heat for 3-5 mins until the sugar dissolves, then pour over the cucumbers and leave to pickle in the fridge while you prepare the tofu.

STEP 2

Heat all but 1 tbsp of the oil in a large, non-stick frying pan over a medium heat until bubbles begin to rise to the surface. Add the tofu and fry for 7-10 mins, turning halfway, until the tofu is evenly golden brown. Remove from the pan and set aside on kitchen paper. In a small bowl, whisk together the honey and miso. Spread the sesame seeds out on a plate. Brush the fried tofu with the sticky honey sauce and set aside any leftovers. Coat the tofu evenly in the seeds, sprinkle with a little salt and leave in a warm place.

STEP 3

Cook the noodles following pack instructions, then drain and rinse in cold water. Return the frying pan to the heat, toss the noodles with the rest of the oil, the remaining sauce and 1 tbsp of the cucumber pickling liquid. Cook for 3 mins until warmed through. Divide the noodles between bowls and top with the tofu, bundles of cucumber and the spring onion.

Fruit leather

Prep: 10 mins **Cook:** 3 hrs - 6 hrs

Makes 1 large sheet (about 10 rolls)

Ingredients

- 400g strawberries or blackberries, fresh or frozen, stalks removed

- 1 dessert apple , core removed and cut into chunks

Method

STEP 1

Tip the strawberries and apple into a saucepan. Put the pan over a low heat, you don't need to add any water. If you've used frozen fruit, juice will run out as they thaw. Heat gently, keeping an eye on the pan until the strawberries start to break down, you can put a lid on the pan if you like, this keeps the steam in and helps the fruit break down. Cook until the strawberries have softened and given up their juice and the apple is soft.

STEP 2

Take the pan off the heat. Purée the contents with a stick blender or in a food processor. Squeeze the purée through a sieve into a clean pan, pushing as much pulp through as possible.

STEP 3

Put the pan back on a low heat and cook, stirring occasionally, until the purée thickens enough to leave a clear patch on the base of the pan when you pull a spoon through it. The more moisture you drive off now, the shorter your drying time will be.

STEP 4

Heat the oven to as low as it will go. Pour the purée onto a lined baking sheet (we use a reusable silicone tray liner) and spread it out to a thin layer, the purée should be thick enough to look opaque.

STEP 5

Put the tray in the oven and dry until the surface is no longer tacky when you touch it, but the leather is still flexible – don't overcook it or it will turn brittle. This will take several hours depending on the oven temperature. If it is very hot and sunny you can air-dry the leather, or use a dehydrator.

STEP 6

Leave the leather to cool to warm and then peel it carefully off the tray. Trim off the raggedy edges. Roll the leather up, then cut the roll into sections, using scissors is easiest. Each of these will unroll to make a strip. Keep the strips individually wrapped and airtight. The offcuts can be chopped up and used in baking, or snacked on.

Easy bread rolls

Prep: 30 mins **Cook:** 25 mins - 30 mins

Makes 8

Ingredients

- 500g strong white bread flour , plus extra for dusting
- 7g sachet fast action yeast
- 1 tsp white caster sugar
- 2 tsp fine salt
- 1 tsp sunflower oil , plus extra for the work surface and bowl

Method

STEP 1

Tip the flour, yeast, sugar, salt and oil into a bowl. Pour over 325ml warm water, then mix (with a spatula or your hand), until it comes together as a shaggy dough. Make sure all the flour has been incorporated. Cover and leave for 10 mins.

STEP 2

Lightly oil your work surface and tip the dough onto it. Knead the dough for at least 10 mins until it becomes tighter and springy – if you have a stand mixer you can do this with a dough hook for 5 mins. Pull the dough into a ball and put in a clean, oiled bowl. Leave for 1 hr, or until doubled in size.

STEP 3

Tip the dough onto a lightly floured surface and roll into a long sausage shape. Halve the dough, then divide each half into four pieces, so you have eight equal-sized portions. Roll each into a tight ball and put on a dusted baking tray, leaving some room between each ball for rising. Cover with a damp tea towel and leave in a warm place to prove for 40 mins-1 hr or until almost doubled in size.

STEP 4

Heat the oven to 230C/210C fan/gas 8. When the dough is ready, dust each ball with a bit more flour. (If you like, you can glaze the rolls with milk or beaten egg, and top with seeds.) Bake for

25-30mins, until light brown and hollow sounding when tapped on the base. Leave to cool on a wire rack.

Raspberry tea ice lollies

Prep: 10 mins plus 4 hrs freezing

Serves 6

Ingredients

- 100g raspberries
- 3 raspberry teabag
- 1 tbsp maple syrup
- juice of 1 lime

Method

STEP 1

Put the raspberries, raspberry tea bags and maple syrup in a bowl, then pour over 350ml boiling water. Leave to infuse for 10 mins, then remove the tea bags, stir in the lime juice and leave to cool. Pour into six ice lolly moulds and freeze for at least 4 hrs, or overnight.

Piccalilli potato salad

Prep: 25 mins **Cook:** 15 mins

plus 2 hrs pickling and cooling

Serves 6

Ingredients

- 750g new potatoes , halved
- ½ small cauliflower (about 350g), broken into very small florets
- 100g green beans , trimmed and halved
- sunflower oil , for frying
- 300g piccalilli
- 3 tbsp olive oil

- 8 radishes, quartered
- 3 baby cucumber, thickly sliced

For the pickled onions

- 100ml cider vinegar
- 2 tbsp sugar
- 1 tsp brown mustard seeds
- 1 large red onion or 2 small, finely sliced

Method

STEP 1

First, make the pickled onions. Pour the vinegar and 50ml water into a small saucepan. Add the sugar, 1 tsp salt and the mustard seeds and simmer over a medium heat, stirring occasionally until the sugar has dissolved. Put half the onion into a heatproof bowl and pour the hot liquid over. Leave to cool slightly, then cover and leave to pickle in the fridge for 2 hrs.

STEP 2

Bring a large pan of salted water to the boil and cook the potatoes for 10 mins. Add the cauliflower and beans, and cook for 2 mins more, then drain.

STEP 3

Heat a depth of 3cm sunflower oil in a small heavy-based saucepan until a small cube of bread dropped into the oil turns golden within 20 seconds. Carefully drop the rest of the onion into the oil and fry for 1-2 mins, or until golden and crisp. Transfer to a sheet of kitchen paper and sprinkle with salt – this will help keep the onions crisp.

STEP 4

Mix the piccalilli and olive oil together in a bowl. Toss with the cooked potatoes, cauliflower and beans, along with the radishes and cucumbers. Toss in the pickled onions, then tip into a serving bowl and top with the crispy onions.

Miso roasted tofu with sweet potato

Prep: 15 mins **Cook:** 30 mins

Serves 2

Ingredients

- 400g firm tofu , drained
- 100g fine green beans
- 2 tbsp vegetable oil
- 2 tbsp black or white sesame seeds , toasted
- 2 large sweet potatoes
- 2 spring onions , finely sliced

For the dressing

- 3 tbsp white miso (if you can't find it, use 2 tbsp brown miso paste)
- 3 tbsp mirin
- 3 tbsp lime juice

Method

STEP 1

Heat oven to 200C/180C fan/gas 6. Wrap the tofu in kitchen paper, place in a shallow dish and put a heavy plate on top to help squeeze out the water. When the paper is wet, replace with another wrapping and weigh down again. Chop the tofu into medium cubes (about 2.5cm). In a small bowl, mix the dressing together with a whisk.

STEP 2

Boil the beans for 1 min, then drain, rinse in cold water and set aside. Line a baking tray with parchment, spread out the tofu and pour over half the dressing. Sprinkle the sesame seeds on top and mix well. Bake for 20-25 mins until golden and crisp. Meanwhile, cut the sweet potatoes in half, place in a bowl, cover with cling film and microwave for 10-15 mins until very soft.

STEP 3

Mash the sweet potato and serve in bowls with the tofu, green beans, the dressing poured over and some spring onions sprinkled on top.

Carrot & cumin hummus with swirled harissa

Prep: 5 mins **Cook:** 40 mins

Serves 8

Ingredients

- 600g carrots
- 2 tbsp olive oil
- 1 tsp cumin seeds
- 1 garlic bulb
- juice of 1 lemon
- 120ml extra virgin olive oil
- 400g can of chickpeas, drained and rinsed
- rose harissa
- flatbreads, to serve

Method

STEP 1

Heat oven to 200C/180C fan/gas 6. Cut 600g carrots into chunks and toss with 2 tbsp olive oil, 1 tsp cumin seeds and a garlic bulb, broken into cloves. Spread onto a baking tray and roast in the oven for 40 mins or until caramelised.

STEP 2

Squeeze the cloves out of their skins and tip into a food processor with the carrots, juice of 1 lemon, 120ml extra virgin olive oil, the drained and rinsed chickpeas, and some seasoning. Blitz until smooth. Swirl through some spicy rose harissa. Serve with flatbreads.

Pea-camole

Prep: 10 mins

Serves 8

Ingredients

- 200g frozen peas
- 2 ripe avocados, halved, stoned and peeled
- 2 limes, juiced
- small bunch coriander

Method

STEP 1

Boil the kettle. Tip the peas into a mixing bowl and cover with about 2.5cm of boiling water. Leave for 5 mins to defrost, then drain well and tip back into the bowl.

STEP 2

Add the avocados with the lime juice and some salt, and mash everything together. Roughly chop the coriander and briefly mash through before serving.

Artichoke & aubergine rice

Prep: 15 mins **Cook:** 50 mins

Serves 6

Ingredients

- 60ml olive oil
- 2 aubergines , cut into chunks
- 1 large onion , finely chopped
- 2 garlic cloves , crushed
- small pack parsley , leaves picked, stalks finely chopped
- 2 tsp smoked paprika
- 2 tsp turmeric
- 400g paella rice
- 1 ½l Kallo vegetable stock
- 2 x 175g packs chargrilled artichokes
- 2 lemons 1 juiced, 1 cut into wedges to serve

Method

STEP 1

Heat 2 tbsp of the oil in a large non-stick frying pan or paella pan. Fry the aubergines until nicely coloured on all sides (add another tbsp of oil if the aubergine begins catching too much), then remove and set aside. Add another tbsp of oil to the pan and lightly fry the onion for 2-3 mins or until softened. Add the garlic and parsley stalks, cook for a few mins more, then stir in the spices and rice until everything is well coated. Heat for 2 mins, add half the stock and cook, uncovered, over a medium heat for 20 mins, stirring occasionally to prevent it from sticking.

STEP 2

Nestle the aubergine and artichokes into the mixture, pour over the rest of the stock and cook for 20 mins more or until the rice is cooked through. Chop the parsley leaves, stir through with the lemon juice and season well. Bring the whole pan to the table and spoon into bowls, with the lemon wedges on the side.

Really easy roasted red pepper sauce

Prep: 10 mins **Cook:** 1 hr

8 (or 2 meals for 4)

Ingredients

- 4 red peppers (or a mix of red, orange and yellow), cut into chunks
- 2 onions , roughly chopped
- 2 garlic cloves (skin left on)
- 2 tbsp olive oil
- 2 x 400g cans peeled plum tomatoes
- 2 tsp red wine vinegar
- 1 tsp light soft brown sugar

Method

STEP 1

Heat oven to 190C/170C fan/gas 5. Toss the peppers and onions with the garlic and olive oil, and spread out in a roasting tin. Roast for 40 mins, then add the tomatoes, red wine vinegar and sugar, and roast for another 20 mins. Tip into a food processor and blend until smooth. Season to taste.

Vegan coleslaw

Prep: 35 mins

Serves 8

Ingredients

- 1 celeriac , about 750g, sliced into thin matchsticks

- 2 large carrots , sliced into thin matchsticks
- 4 spring onions , very finely sliced
- 2 bok choi , shredded
- 200g frozen peas , cooked and cooled
- handful flat-leaf parsley , chopped
- handful coriander , chopped
- For the dressing
- juice ½ lime
- 3 tbsp sunflower oil , groundnut or corn oil
- 2 tbsp white wine vinegar

Method

STEP 1

Put the dressing ingredients into a bowl, whisk well, then set aside. The dressing can be made a day ahead. Mix together the celeriac, carrots, spring onions, bok choy and peas. Sprinkle with a little salt, mix again and leave to stand for 5 mins.

STEP 2

Pour the dressing over the vegetables and mix well. Stir in the parsley and coriander just before serving.

Rice & peas

Prep: 5 mins **Cook:** 20 mins

Serves 4 as a side

Ingredients

- 400g can kidney beans , rinsed and drained
- 400ml can low-fat coconut milk
- ½ tsp dried thyme
- ½ tsp ground allspice
- 6 spring onions , sliced
- 200g long grain rice

Method

STEP 1

Put the beans, coconut milk, thyme, allspice, 4 of the spring onions and 100ml water in a pan, and bring to a simmer. Season with plenty of salt and black pepper.

STEP 2

Rinse the rice a few times in a sieve until the water runs clear. Tip into the pan and simmer for 10 mins over a medium heat, stirring occasionally, before lowering the heat. Put the lid on and cook for another 5 mins until the grains are tender and the liquid has been absorbed. Fluff up the rice with a fork before serving and scatter with the reserved spring onions.

Homemade sourdough bread

Prep: 1 hr **Cook:** 40 mins

Plus 7 days for the starter and at least 6 hrs rising

Makes 1 loaf (cuts into 10 slices)

Ingredients

For the sourdough starter

- 50g strong white flour to start, then 25g extra a day for 6 days
- 50g strong wholemeal flour to start, then 25g extra a day for 6 days
- For the sourdough loaf
- 450g strong white flour , plus extra for dusting
- 50g wholemeal flour
- 10g fine salt
- 100g sourdough starter (see above)

Method

STEP 1

To make the sourdough starter, whisk 50g strong white flour and 50g strong wholemeal flour with 100ml slightly warm water until smooth. Transfer to a large jar or plastic container. Leave the lid ajar for 1 hr or so in a warm place, then seal and set aside for 24 hrs. For the next six days, you will need to 'feed' it. Each day, tip away half the original starter, add an extra 25g of each flour and 50ml slightly warm water, and stir well. After a few days, you should start to see bubbles on the surface, and it will smell yeasty. On day seven, the starter should be bubbly and smell much sweeter. It is now ready to be used, but make sure you keep half back and carry on feeding for your next loaf.

STEP 2

Tip both the flours, 300ml warm water and the starter into a bowl, stir with a wooden spoon into a dough and leave somewhere for an hour.

STEP 3

Tip in 25ml more water and the salt and bring everything together. Cover and leave somewhere warm for 3 hrs, folding the dough onto itself several times in the first hour. The dough should increase in size by about a third.

STEP 4

Line a medium bowl with a clean tea towel and flour it really well, or flour a proving basket. Tip the dough back onto your work surface, shape into a tight, smooth ball and dust it with flour.

STEP 5

Place the dough, seam-side up, in the bowl or proving basket, and leave at room temperature for 3 hrs – or better still in the fridge overnight – until risen by about a quarter.

STEP 6

Heat oven to 230C/210C fan/gas 8 and put a casserole dish with a lid or a baking stone in the oven for at least 30 mins to heat up, and a large roasting tin filled with boiling water underneath. After 30 mins, carefully remove the casserole dish, invert the loaf into it and slash the top. Cover and bake for 20 mins, then take the lid off and bake for another 20 mins. Or invert onto the baking stone, slash and bake for 40 mins, or until the crust is as dark as you like it.

Sizzled sprouts with pistachios & pomegranate

Prep: 10 mins **Cook:** 20 mins

Serves 8

Ingredients

- 3 tbsp olive oil

- 500g Brussels sprouts, halved
- 50g pistachios, roughly chopped
- 100g pomegranate seeds
- pomegranate molasses, to drizzle (optional)

Method

STEP 1

Heat the oil in a large frying pan over a medium-high heat. Put the sprouts in the pan, cut-side down, and leave them to fry for 10-15 mins, tossing occasionally. If they're just lightly brown, carry on cooking for a further 5 mins until blistered.

STEP 2

Scatter over the pistachios and stir-fry until toasted. Remove from the heat and stir through the pomegranate seeds. Season with salt and tip into a serving dish. Drizzle with a little pomegranate molasses, if you like.

Summer porridge

Prep: 20 mins

Serves 2

Ingredients

- 300ml almond milk
- 200g blueberries
- ½ tbsp maple syrup
- 2 tbsp chia seeds
- 100g jumbo oats
- 1 kiwi fruit, cut into slices
- 50g pomegranate seeds
- 2 tsp mixed seeds

Method

STEP 1

In a blender, blitz the milk, blueberries and maple syrup until the milk turns purple. Put the chia and oats in a mixing bowl, pour in the blueberry milk and stir very well. Leave to soak for 5 mins, stirring occasionally, until the liquid has absorbed, and the oats and chia thicken and swell.

STEP 2

Stir again, then divide between two bowls. Arrange the fruit on top, then sprinkle over the mixed seeds. Will keep in the fridge for 1 day. Add the toppings just before serving.

Miso soup

Prep: 10 mins **Cook:** 5 mins

Serves 4 as a starter or snack

Ingredients

- 5g dried wakame seaweed
- 1l dashi (shop bought or see tip)
- 200g fresh silken tofu , or firm if you prefer, cut into 1cm cubes
- 2 tbsp white miso paste
- 3 tbsp red miso paste
- spring onion , finely chopped, to serve

Method

STEP 1

Put the wakame in a small bowl and cover with cold water, then leave it for 5 mins until the leaves have fully expanded.

STEP 2

Make the dashi (see tip below) or heat until it reaches a rolling boil. Add the tofu and cook for 1 min before adding the seaweed.

STEP 3

Reduce the heat. Put both types of miso in a ladle or strainer and dip it into the pot. Slowly loosen up the miso with a spoon inside the ladle or strainer; the paste will slowly melt into the dashi. Once all the miso is dissolved into the soup, turn off the heat immediately. Sprinkle with chopped spring onions to add colour and fragrance.

Miso ramen

Prep: 10 mins **Cook:** 15 mins

Serves 4

Ingredients

- 5 tbsp miso paste
- 2 tbsp soy sauce
- 2.5cm piece ginger , grated
- 12 shiitake mushrooms
- 225g smoked tofu , cut into 4 slices
- 2 tbsp liquid aminos or tamari
- 250g soba noodles
- 16 ears baby corn
- 1 tbsp vegetable oil
- 8 baby pak choi
- 200g ready-to-eat beansprouts (if they're not labelled ready-to-eat, cook thoroughly until steaming hot throughout)
- 2 red chillies , finely sliced on an angle
- 2 spring onions , finely sliced on an angle
- 4 tbsp crispy seaweed
- 2 tbsp black sesame seeds
- 1 tbsp sesame oil , to finish

Method

STEP 1

Put the miso, 1.5 litres water, soy sauce, ginger and shiitake in a large saucepan. Stir to mix in the miso, then bring to a very gentle simmer. Keep simmering for 5 mins.

STEP 2

Meanwhile, place the smoked tofu in a shallow bowl and pour over the liquid aminos. Turn the tofu slices over to make sure they are soaked well on both sides.

STEP 3

Bring a pan of salted water to the boil. Add the soba noodles, bring back to the boil and cook until just tender, about 5 mins.

STEP 4

Add the baby corn to the miso broth and cook for a further 4 mins.

STEP 5

Meanwhile, heat the oil in a non-stick frying pan over a high heat. Lift the tofu from its bowl, shaking off the excess liquid aminos and saving it. Gently place the tofu in the frying pan and cook for 2-3 mins on each side until browned. Add the reserved liquid aminos to the pan (it will bubble up) and reduce to a glaze. Remove from the heat.

STEP 6

As soon as the noodles are cooked, drain them in a colander and rinse under cold water, then divide between four serving bowls. Add the pak choi to the miso broth and remove from the heat.

STEP 7

Divide the pak choi, baby corn and beansprouts between the bowls. Ladleover the miso broth and add the tofu. Garnish with the chillies, spring onions and crispy seaweed. Sprinkle with sesame seeds, drizzle over the sesame oil and serve straightaway.

Root veg lentil bowl with herb pistou

Prep:30 mins **Cook:**50 mins

Serves 4

Ingredients

- 600g leftover root veg (carrots and parsnips work well)
- 1 tbsp rose harissa
- 3 tbsp rapeseed oil
- 150g baby spinach
- ½ small bunch of coriander
- ½ small bunch of mint

- 1 small garlic clove
- 30g mixed nuts , toasted and cooled
- 1 lemon , zested and juiced
- cooked puy lentils (or 2 x 250g pouches)

Method

STEP 1

Heat the oven to 200C/180C fan/gas 6. Slice the carrots into chunks, or halve lengthways if they are small, and quarter the parsnips lengthways. Toss with the harissa and ½ tbsp oil and season. Tip onto a baking tray and roast for 40-45 mins or until tender. Toss the spinach and 1 tbsp of water through for the last 5 mins to wilt.

STEP 2

Blitz the remaining oil, the coriander, mint, garlic and nuts in a food processor until smooth – add 1 tbsp water if needed. Season and stir in the lemon zest and juice.

STEP 3

Warm the lentils through in the microwave or in a pan with a few tablespoons of water, then toss with the roots and spinach. Spoon into bowls and top with the herb pistou.

Pitta bread

Prep:20 mins **Cook:**40 mins

Makes 8

Ingredients

- 2 tsp fast-action dried yeast
- 500g strong white bread flour, plus extra for dusting
- 2 tsp salt
- 1 tbsp olive oil

Method

STEP 1

Mix the yeast with 300ml warm water in a large bowl. Leave to sit for 5 mins until the yeast is super bubbly then tip in the flour, salt and olive oil. Bring the mixture together into a soft dough. Don't worry if it looks a little rough round the edges.

STEP 2

Tip the dough onto a lightly floured work surface. Knead for 5-10 mins until you have a soft, smooth and elastic dough. Try to knead using as little extra flour as possible, just enough so that the dough doesn't stick – this will keep the pittas light and airy. Once kneaded, place in a lightly oiled bowl, cover with a tea towel and leave to double in size, approximately 1 hour.

STEP 3

Heat oven as high as it will go (ideally 250C/230C fan/gas 9) and put a large baking tray on the middle shelf of the oven to get searingly hot. Divide the dough into eight balls then flatten each into a disc with the palm of your hand. On a lightly floured surface, roll each disc into an oval, around 20cm long, 15cm wide and 3-5mm thick.

STEP 4

Carefully remove the hot tray from the oven. Dust with flour then place your pittas directly onto it – you may have to do this in batches. Return swiftly to the oven and bake for 4-5 mins, or until the pittas have puffed up and are a pale golden colour. Wrap each hot pitta in a clean tea towel once it's baked to keep it soft while the others cook.

Cardamom & peach quinoa porridge

Prep: 3 mins **Cook:** 20 mins

Serves 2

Ingredients

- 75g quinoa
- 25g porridge oats
- 4 cardamom pods
- 250ml unsweetened almond milk
- 2 ripe peaches , cut into slices
- 1 tsp maple syrup

Method

STEP 1

Put the quinoa, oats and cardamom pods in a small saucepan with 250ml water and 100ml of the almond milk. Bring to the boil, then simmer gently for 15 mins, stirring occasionally.

STEP 2

Pour in the remaining almond milk and cook for 5 mins more until creamy.

STEP 3

Remove the cardamom pods, spoon into bowls or jars, and top with the peaches and maple syrup.

Fajita seasoning

Prep: 5 mins

Makes 1 small jar

Ingredients

- ½ tbsp hot chilli powder
- 2 tbsp sweet smoked paprika
- 1 tbsp ground cumin
- 1 tbsp garlic powder
- ½ tbsp ground coriander
- 1 heaped tbsp dried oregano

Method

STEP 1

Put all the ingredients in a bowl and mix to combine. Tip into a small jar or container and store in a dark, cool place. Use as you wish, adding 1 tsp at a time to a dish according to taste.

Next level ratatouille

Prep: 20 mins **Cook:** 2 hrs

Serves 6

Ingredients

- 3 red peppers, each quartered and deseeded
- handful basil, leaves and stalks separated
- large thyme sprig
- 2 tbsp olive oil, plus extra for frying and drizzling
- 2 courgettes (different colours are good), roughly chopped
- 1 aubergine, chopped into large chunks
- 1 red onion, roughly chopped
- 4 garlic cloves, sliced
- pinch sugar
- 1 tbsp red wine vinegar
- 2 x 400g cans cherry tomatoes
- 1 tbsp extra virgin olive oil

- griddled sourdough, to serve

Method

STEP 1

Heat the grill to high. Lay the pepper quarters skin-side up on a baking tray and grill until the skins are black and charred. Tip into a bowl, cover and leave to cool. Peel the charred skin off the peppers, then cut into strips, and toss back in the juices collected in the bowl. Tie the basil stalks and thyme sprig together using kitchen string and set aside.

STEP 2

Heat the oven to 160C/140C fan/ gas 4. Heat the olive oil in a flameproof casserole dish and fry the courgettes and aubergine for 15 mins until nicely browned. You may need to do this in batches, adding more oil to the pan as needed so the pan is never dry.

STEP 3

Scoop the veg out of the pan and set aside. Add a drizzle more oil, tip in the onion and cook for another 15 mins until softened and starting to brown. Add the garlic and leave to sizzle for a moment. Scatter with sugar, then leave for a minute to caramelise and splash in the vinegar. Stir in the cooked vegetables along with the pepper juice, season generously, pour over the cans of tomatoes and bring everything to a simmer.

STEP 4

Nestle in the herbs, cover the dish and transfer to the oven for 1 hr. Remove the lid and give it another 30 mins until everything is cooked down and jammy. Leave the ratatouille to cool until just warm, then stir through most of the basil leaves and the extra virgin olive oil. Scatter with the rest of the basil and serve with griddled sourdough.

Spiced mushroom & lentil hotpot

Prep: 10 mins **Cook:** 35 mins

Serves 4

Ingredients

- 2 tbsp olive oil
- 1 medium onion, sliced
- 300g mini Portobello mushrooms or chestnut mushrooms, sliced
- 2 garlic cloves, crushed
- 1 ½ tsp ground cumin
- 1 tsp smoked paprika
- 2 x 400g cans green lentils, drained and rinsed (drained weight 240g)
- 1 tbsp soy sauce
- 1 tbsp balsamic vinegar
- 1 medium sweet potato, peeled and very thinly sliced
- 1 large potato, very thinly sliced
- 1 thyme sprig, leaves picked

Method

STEP 1

Heat oven to 200C/180C fan/gas 6. Heat half the oil in a medium saucepan. Fry the onion for 3 mins, then add the mushrooms. Cook for another 3 mins, then increase the heat and add the garlic, ground cumin and paprika, and cook for 1 min. Remove from the heat and add the lentils, soy sauce, balsamic vinegar and 100ml water. Season, then tip the mixture into a casserole dish.

STEP 2

Rinse the saucepan and return to the hob. Add a kettle full of boiled water and bring back to the boil over a high heat. Add the potato slices, cook for 3 mins, then drain. Arrange on top of the lentils, then brush with the remaining oil. Roast in the oven for 25 mins until the potatoes are golden, then scatter over the thyme before serving.

Tofu brekkie pancakes

Prep: 10 mins **Cook:** 10 mins

Serves 4 - 6

Ingredients

- 50g Brazil nuts
- 3 sliced bananas
- 240g raspberries
- maple syrup or honey , to serve
- For the batter
- 349g pack firm silken tofu
- 2 tsp vanilla extract
- 2 tsp lemon juice
- 400ml unsweetened almond milk
- 1 tbsp vegetable oil , plus 1-2 tbsp extra for frying
- 250g buckwheat flour
- 4 tbsp light muscovado sugar
- 1 ½ tsp ground mixed spice
- 1 tbsp gluten-free baking powder

Method

STEP 1

Heat oven to 180C/160C fan/gas 4. Scatter the nuts over a baking tray and cook for 5 mins until toasty and golden. Leave to cool, then chop. Turn the oven down low if you want to keep the whole batch of pancakes warm, although I think they are best enjoyed straight from the pan.

STEP 2

Put the tofu, vanilla, lemon juice and 200ml of the milk into a deep jug or bowl. Using a stick blender, blend together until liquid, then keep going until it turns thick and smooth, like yogurt. Stir in the oil and the rest of the milk to loosen the mixture.

STEP 3

Put the dry ingredients and 1 tsp salt in a large bowl and whisk to combine and aerate. If there are any lumps in the sugar, squish them with your fingers. Make a well in the centre, pour in the tofu mix and bring together to make a thick batter.

STEP 4

Heat a large (ideally non-stick) frying pan and swirl around 1 tsp oil. For golden pancakes that don't stick, the pan and oil should be hot enough to get an enthusiastic sizzle on contact with the batter, but not so hot that it scorches it. Test a drop.

STEP 5

Using a ladle or large serving spoon, drop in 3 spoonfuls of batter, easing it out gently in the pan to make pancakes that are about 12cm across. Cook for 2 mins on the first side or until bubbles pop over most of the surface. Loosen with a palette knife, then flip over the pancakes and cook for 1 min more or until puffed up and firm. Transfer to the oven to keep warm, if you need to, but don't stack the pancakes too closely. Cook the rest of the batter, using a little more oil each time. Serve warm with sliced banana, berries, toasted nuts and a good drizzle of maple syrup or honey.

Sunshine lollies

Prep: 20 mins

makes 6 x 60ml lollies

Ingredients

- 5 large carrots
- juice of 3 large oranges , zest of 1
- 1 satsuma , peeled then chopped (optional)

Method

STEP 1

Finely grate the carrots and place in the middle of a clean tea towel. Gather up the towel, and squeeze the carrot juice into a jug, discarding the pulp. Add the orange juice and top up with a little cold water if needed to make up 360ml liquid. Stir in the orange zest and satsuma pieces, if using. Pour into lolly moulds and freeze overnight.

Roasted squash & red onion with pistachios

Prep: 15 mins **Cook:** 25 mins

Serves 4

Ingredients

- 1 large butternut squash, peeled, ends trimmed, halved widthways and spiralized into thick noodles
- 1 large red onion, peeled, ends trimmed and spiralized using the ribbon attachment
- 2 tbsp olive oil
- 2 tsp sumac
- 50g pomegranate seeds
- 30g pistachios, toasted and roughly chopped

Method

STEP 1

Heat oven to 200C/180C fan/gas 6. Toss the spiralized butternut squash and onion together with the oil, sumac, some sea salt and black pepper in a roasting tray. Spread out then roast for 25 mins until the vegetables are completely tender and beginning to caramelize.

STEP 2

Divide between plates and top with the pomegranate seeds and toasted pistachios.

Savoury spiced granola

Prep: 10 mins **Cook:** 30 mins

Serves 15-20

Ingredients

- 350g jumbo oats
- 100g mixed seeds
- 80g peanuts
- 250g canned chickpeas
- 1 ½ tsp chilli flakes

- 2 tsp turmeric
- 2 tsp ground cumin
- 2 tsp crushed coriander seeds
- 2 heaped tsp flaked sea salt
- 80ml rapeseed oil

Method

STEP 1

Heat oven to 180C/160C fan/gas 4. Toss together the oats, mixed seeds, peanuts, chickpeas (after draining them and patting them dry) in an oven tray along with the chilli flakes, turmeric, ground cumin, crushed coriander seeds and flaked sea salt. Stir through the rapeseed oil. Bake for 25-30 mins or until lightly golden and crunchy, stirring halfway. Leave to cool completely before storing (see below). Sprinkle over salads and soups.

Beetroot hummus party platter

Prep: 15 mins

Serves 8

Ingredients

- 2 x 400g can chickpeas , drained
- 2 x 300g pack cooked beetroot , drained
- 2 small garlic cloves
- 2 tbsp tahini
- 100ml extra virgin olive oil , plus a drizzle to serve
- good squeeze of lemon juice
- 2 tbsp toasted hazelnuts , roughly chopped
- 2 tbsp pumpkin seeds , roughly chopped
- 2 tsp nigella seeds
- 1 tsp sumac (optional)
- pinch of chilli flakes (optional)

To serve (optional)

- crunchy summer veg , cut into batons (we used fennel, sugar snap peas, baby heritage carrots & radishes)

- bread, toasted and cut into fingers for dipping
- mini mozzarella balls
- olives
- prosciutto-wrapped breadsticks

Method

STEP 1

Set about 2 tbsp chickpeas aside. Tip the rest of the chickpeas, the beetroot, garlic, tahini, oil and lemon juice into a food processor with a good pinch of salt. Blend until smooth, then check the seasoning, adding a little more salt or lemon if it needs it. Chill the hummus until you're ready to serve (it will keep for up to two days).

STEP 2

Transfer the hummus to a wide, shallow bowl or spread over a platter. Drizzle with some oil, scatter with the reserved chickpeas, hazelnuts, seeds, sumac and chilli (if using). Arrange the crunchy veg and other accompaniments around the platter and let everyone dig in.

Printed in Great Britain
by Amazon